Reviews for *Beyond Charity*

DeBorah Gilbert White offers us a heartbreaking, heart-challenging memoir – a compelling reminder that none of us are immune to housing insecurity. Through powerful storytelling and astute systems analysis, she courageously shares her lived experience to draw others into understanding, questioning, and ultimately changing, structural barriers that make and keep people homeless. In *Beyond Charity*, her vulnerability becomes an invitation to love and understand our neighbors more compassionately and to respond more justly. This book may have started as a gift to herself, as she notes in its opening pages, but in truth, it will become a gift of grace and light to every reader.

—The **Rev. Dr. J. Bennett Guess**, Executive Director, ACLU of Ohio, United Church of Christ (UCC)

***

Dr. Gilbert White speaks with an authentic voice about coping with experiencing homelessness and being a voice for the vulnerable and voiceless. Her homeless advocacy work in the community shines a light on the homeless industrial complex and homeless services systemic issues. Her work for a Bill of Rights for Persons Experiencing Homelessness in Delaware brings deeper focus to societal perceptions about poverty, people identified as poor, the unhoused, and the issue of housing Justice. ***Beyond Charity: A Sojourner's Reflections on Homelessness, Advocacy,***

DeBorah Gilbert White, PhD.

Empowerment and Hope is a powerful story that takes the reader step by step on one woman's journey of empowerment to bring about social change. DeBorah is an advocate, organizer, educator, woman of faith, comrade, sister, and friend.

—**Chaplain Deborah Dickerson**, member Picture the Homeless, New York City Coalition Continuum of Care, Board of East Harlem El Barrio Community Land Trust, National Alliance to End Homelessness, Board Poor Peoples Campaign for Equity and Human Rights, National Low Income Housing Coalition, and formerly homeless.

***

Beyond Charity: A Sojourner's Reflections on Homelessness, Advocacy, Empowerment and Hope by Dr. DeBorah Gilbert White is much more powerful than just reflections on homelessness. It is a "Call to Action." Those of us who are compassionate, spiritual beings, must become activists, to ensure that our people are living in safe, affordable housing. She points out that the propaganda about the homeless population has been created to elicit both a lack of empathy and a lack of action. We must correct this inhumane condition that impacts over 2.5 million children, with another 15% of the population in each state struggling with housing insecurity. Our preconceived notions of homelessness are not accidental and are challenged in Dr. Gilbert White's book. Over half of those who are homeless are Melanics (People of Color). Her book is a frightening reminder that those of us who live in comfortable homes could become homeless overnight, due to a myriad of circumstances, including mental illness, COVID-19, ageism, and racism. Dr. Gilbert White is a dedicated advocate who presents a compelling statement about why and how the United States of America must make housing our people — and passing a bill of rights for the homeless — a priority. Everyone deserves housing!

—**Dr. Ayo Maria Gooden**, President Delaware Valley Association of Black Psychologists

***

I am honored to recommend DeBorah Gilbert White's book. DeBorah is a fantastic leader, and her brilliant and charismatic leadership is phenomenal. I have known DeBorah for almost a decade and have witnessed her relentless work ethic and passion for abolishing homelessness and internalized racism.

Through her own experience of triumph over incredible obstacles, DeBorah exemplifies the value of perseverance and persistence. Her work has personally moved many people. I am proud to call DeBorah a dear friend. Her works have changed countless lives and continue as we speak. I fully endorse ***Beyond Charity: A Sojourner's Reflections on Homelessness, Advocacy, Empowerment and Hope*** for all those wanting inspiration and a road map to changing the lives of people experiencing homelessness.

—**Donald H. Whitehead Jr**. Executive Director
National Coalition for the Homeless, Washington, D.C.

***

Most of us are witness to a growing crisis of housing and food insecurity in the United States. People are made vulnerable through any number of factors: discrimination, layoffs, relationships ending, loss of affordable housing through gentrification and rising cost of living, exploitation of low-wage workers, and the precarity of adjunct teaching. But few of us are so determined as Dr. Gilbert White to refuse to settle for bandages over prevention.

Dr. Gilbert White generously shares her story as a view into the broader narrative of the crisis of those experiencing houselessness in the United States. Her story adeptly raises complex issues, including how our society is invested in continuing the crisis of homelessness. She turns her own experience into fuel to work on behalf of everyone who does or might experience homelessness and shares how a community of people engages in policy advocacy, tenants' rights organizing, human rights, individual empowerment, and ultimately prevention. For those of us who belong to religious communities purporting to be committed to justice for all, this book invites us to share in the fight for real change and will energize us with possibilities for a world-oriented towards human rights.

—The Reverend Laura Mariko Cheifetz, Presbyterian Church (USA).

Beyond Charity:

A Sojourner's Reflections on Homelessness, Advocacy, Empowerment and Hope

DeBorah Gilbert White, PhD.

Published by KHARIS PUBLISHING, imprint of KHARIS MEDIA LLC.

Copyright © 2021 DeBorah Gilbert White, PhD.

ISBN-13: 978-1-63746-073-3
ISBN-10: 1-63746-073-2

Library of Congress Control Number: 2021943366

All rights reserved. This book or parts thereof may not be reproduced in any form, stored in a retrieval system, or transmitted in any form by any means - electronic, mechanical, photocopy, recording, or otherwise - without prior written permission of the publisher, except as provided by United States of America copyright law.

All Scripture quotations, unless otherwise indicated, are taken from the Holy Bible, New Revised Standard Version ®, RSV®. Copyright ©1973, 1978, 1984, 2011 by Biblical, Inc.™ Used by permission.

Credit: TOXIC CHARITY by ROBERT D. LUPTON. Copyright (c) 2011 by Robert D. Lupton. Courtesy of HarperCollins Publishers.

All KHARIS PUBLISHING products are available at special quantity discounts for bulk purchase for sales promotions, premiums, fundraising, and educational needs. For details, contact:

Kharis Media LLC
Tel: 1-479-599-8657
support@kharispublishing.com
www.kharispublishing.com

For all who experience homelessness, are formerly homeless, or at risk of homelessness, and the many who advocate for our humanity, dignity, and housing as a human right.

I am no longer accepting the things I cannot change. I am changing the things I cannot accept.

—Dr. Angela Davis

Philanthropy is commendable, but it must not cause the philanthropist to overlook the circumstances of economic injustice which make philanthropy necessary.

—Rev. Dr. Martin Luther King, Jr.

Acknowledgments

The journey of writing this memoir connected me to so many people who were supportive and believed that the story needed to be told. Thank you to my children, Jasmine and Malcolm, who did not think it was "too much" to go deep in bringing my story to the reader. To my mom, Margaret, brother Jeffrey, and sisters, Cassandra and Theodora, thank you for your support and for the role you play in me continually evolving into my authentic self.

A special thank you to a host of friends, acquaintances, and allies who supported me with encouraging words, inspirational cards, monetary donations, valued feedback, and community allyship to spread the advocacy work of HerStory Ensemble LLC; Neighbors In Need Grant of the United Church of Christ, Reverend Jayne Oasin, Barbara Baylor, Judy Richardson, Carol Grannum, Judye Thomas, Kelly Green, Theresa Randall, Akua (MaryAlice Saunders), Siraj (Billy Morgan), Evangelist Carolyn Mauras, Sharon Jefferson, Leann Moore, Fostina Dixon, Dr. Ayo Maria Gooden, Rosemary Davis, Shenandoah Gale, Sherri Akil, Delores Turner, Kelvin Lassiter, Reverend Sheree Hill-Manlove, Dr. Denise Hinds-Zaami, Rhonda Celester, Danielle Deputy, Minnie White, Tanisha Gilbert, Dr. Ann Aviles, Kyra Hoffner, Attorney Daniel Atkins, Jon Hurdle, Donna Fazio, Granville White, Ilene White, Oscar Brashear, Dr. Wanda Evans-Brewer, Stephanie Morris, Chaplain Deborah Dickerson, Attorney Eric Tars, Donald Whitehead, Jazmen Oneal, Zmora Broward, Reverend Laura M. Cheifetz, Iris Oneal, Sherrell Johnson, Reverend Dr. J. Bennett Guess, Shyanne Miller, Emlyn DeGannes, Reverend Belinda M. Curry, Roxanna Farris, Retha Savage, Evelyn

DeBorah Gilbert White, PhD.

Bandoh, Reverend Adora Iris Lee, and the Delaware Valley Association of Black Psychologists.

My final thoughts of appreciation and thanks go to the women of HerStory Ensemble for your advice and guidance on the issues this book brings focus to, and to Marita Golden and the Women Writers of Color Network in Washington, D.C. for inviting me into the circle.

Author's Note

This book is a gift to myself that I share with you. I did not recognize this fact until I finished writing it. Providing a gift to self in this form is appropriate and telling. In essence, this book provided the space for me to share my truth, to speak that truth to power, and to possibly assist others on their journey for social change in some small way. Some of the names in the book have been changed to protect the privacy of others. However, the emphasis on human dignity and social and systemic transformation is lifted loud and clear.

Beyond Charity: A Sojourner's Reflections on Homelessness, Advocacy, Empowerment and Hope is the best gift after the birth of my children Jasmine and Malcolm. They have made life worth living, and are reminders of the importance of moving forward, no matter what it looks like. It is a gift because writing it set me free. I thank God for the vision to utilize my story to help facilitate social justice and social change.

TABLE OF CONTENTS

1	Sheltered Homeless	1
2	Coping	19
3	Underemployed and Evicted	23
4	Transitions	39
5	Permanent Housing	49
6	Next Steps	53
7	Reflections	61
8	Community Activism and Advocacy	67
9	The Politics of Homelessness	71
10	The Homeless Industrial Complex	79
11	HerStory Ensemble	91
12	Beyond Charity	101
13	Empowered for Change	115
14	We Matter	129

Sheltered Homeless

I became homeless. I was homeless. I experienced homelessness. These are the words I use to share that at one time in my life, I did not have my own place to live. Being identified as homeless, I felt that in some way I had failed myself in not being able to keep the promises I had made to self, and to being a positive role model for my children. I never thought it would happen to me. The experience revealed challenges people without housing face living on the streets, in shelters, transitional housing, and doubling up with family and friends. My eyes were opened to how overwhelmed homeless service providers and other outreach organizations addressing homelessness were. I was able to see flaws in systems that impact people without permanent housing. There was also the difference in how homelessness was being defined, and its accompanying myths and stereotypes. I came to understand how responses to homelessness were shaped by the perceptions, attitudes, and fears held by society and individuals about people identified as poor, and particularly those identified as homeless.

I did not have legal representation when I was evicted. A lingering question for me has been: If I had representation in the beginning of the eviction process, would I have been evicted? Often, when talking about the eviction, people would ask if I had read *Evicted*, the book written by Matthew Desmond that shed light on inequities connected to housing. Desmond reminded us of the power imbalance in housing courts, where 90% of landlords are represented, and 90% of tenants are not. I would better understand that imbalance a few years after my eviction when I had to challenge a landlord who would not return my money when I decided not to move into substandard housing. There was a need to expand the narrative about who was homeless, why people became homeless, and to protect the humanity, dignity, and rights of people experiencing homelessness.

I do remember that trying to stay housed was a lonely process, whereas each step along the way taught me about my own personal resolve and Delaware's social services. I was being exposed to a world that was laden with stereotypes, myths, misinformation, and social justice issues. Experiencing homelessness, I was at the mercy of the decisions of others, but I was not oblivious to the covert and overt ways that my humanity and dignity were being chipped away, and how vulnerable I and others were made to feel. This reality placed me on the path to become an advocate.

If homelessness could happen to me, it can happen to anyone. I decided to share my journey and to collaborate with those who have been working for transformative change toward ending homelessness. I believe that we can end it as we have come to know it in the United States through greater preventive measures, like a livable wage, increasing the availability of low-income and affordable housing, and having a right to counsel for tenants going through the eviction process. I see myself as a survivor, and not easily broken by all that life has already thrown my way. I share my journey from homelessness to advocacy to bring awareness, to educate, to facilitate deeper understanding, and to promote change.

As a professional woman, I had traveled the United States extensively. I had traveled to South Africa twice, I had walked the Valleys of the Kings and Queens, and sailed the Nile River in Egypt, visited Mexico, Canada, England, and many of the Caribbean islands. I had owned two homes at one time in my lifetime, living in one and providing housing for a family in the other as rental property. Those experiences now seemed worlds away with life's twists and turns. I was raised to believe that if I did everything that society told me to do, like work hard, get an education, and obey the law, that certain things would not happen to me. But I have come to realize that things do happen, and often those things are out of our control, and none of us are exempt. However, I was now experiencing homelessness. Today, I have memory of my first reckoning with the weakness in thinking that if we only worked hard, success would follow. I learned as a teenager working at a summer job at a toy factory in the Bronx, New York, that simply working hard was not a guarantee for success. At the time, I did not have the depth of social analysis or language to express what I observed and was sensing. Many of the people working at the factory were immigrants. They were working hard every day in a dead-end job in challenging working conditions. Not only were we working hard, but we were doing it standing on our feet all day long. That job convinced me to finish high school and to attend college. The experience taught me that it was not enough to work hard, but it was also important to work smart, and to have access to the opportunities an education prepared you for. Even with that, there was no guarantee that obtaining success would not present challenges and obstacles.

I received the call from social services that a bed would be available for me in the coming week at the Emergency Housing Residence of the Salvation Army in Wilmington, Delaware. The bed was in a fifty-two-bed homeless shelter for women and women with children. I would be there for thirty days, with the option to extend my stay to ninety days, if needed. During my conversations with social services I indicated that I would need to be in a place where I could teach my online class, have freedom to go to teach my on-campus class, and access to my cell phone. I was told this was that place. In the late afternoon of February 7, 2012, I found myself sitting patiently in the shelter's waiting area with a plastic bag containing some of my belongings, and with my laptop computer in its carry bag. Parked across the street from the shelter was my 2004 silver Saturn Ion sedan. It contained a suitcase with more seasonal clothing, a few pairs of shoes and boots, personal care items, boxes with important papers, and books. The back seat was folded down to hold most of these items, which I covered with a large cloth. The front passenger seat held some items as well.

While waiting, I completed some paperwork and then took the elevator with a staff member up to a small room on the third floor that contained three sets of bunk beds. There was no one in the room at the time, although there was evidence of occupancy. I was assigned the top bunk of the set against a wall that had the only window in the room. I had not been on the top bunk of a bunk bed since I was a child. Now, at fifty-four years old, it felt strange to be sleeping on a bunk bed, and in a room with people I did not know. There were combination dresser-closets near each set of beds to place clothing and other personal items. However, none were secure, and I sensed that I would need to keep a watchful eye on my belongings. I hated the thought of having to focus on not having my stuff stolen.

Across from the room was a community bathroom. I was curious and a little anxious about sharing a bathroom with strangers in this setting. Stepping into the bathroom I noticed that there were two showers, one on each side of the room as you entered. As I walked further into the bathroom, there were multiple sinks with mirrors, and toilet stalls with doors. I looked around and thought, it wasn't too bad. I had seen worse. I liked the idea that I did not have to wander far to use the bathroom. Each floor had a common sitting or lounge area. I would discover later it was another space to gather outside the rooms, and to connect with some of the other women in the shelter. It would be in one of these areas where I would settle each night to facilitate my online class. My classes were asynchronous, meaning we didn't all need to be in the classroom at the same time, there was no face-to-face contact, and being in the classroom was not a daily requirement for the students or for myself. This flexibility allowed me to be in the classroom different days and different times during the week. It worked well for the present situation.

I was shown a room with a desktop computer for resident use. People could check emails and do job searches there. I was escorted to the laundry room on another floor to wash the clothes in my bag. Everyone entering the shelter had to wash their clothes. I would learn that this was the process used to control bedbugs. It was the first time I would personally feel the stigma of being homeless as it related to the stereotype of not being clean. The laundry room was down the hall from the shelter's general meeting area, which also served as its cafeteria. I ate something while waiting for my clothes to dry.

Returning to the room I encountered two roommates. "Hi," I said, entering the room, and both replied, "Hi." As I started putting my items away, one asked, "Which bed is yours?" I pointed to the top bunk by the window. I would soon find out her name was Trish. Trish, a twenty-something year old White woman, was assigned to the lower bunk on the opposite wall across from mine. The other roommate, Diane, a thirty-something year old African American woman, was assigned to the lower bunk along the wall adjacent to the window. As I checked the ladder with my hand to climb into bed, Diane shared that there was someone assigned to her top bunk named Brenda, and someone assigned to the bottom bed of my bunk, who she had not seen in a couple of days. It was good that she was giving me a "lay of the land" and I politely smiled at her as I settled on the bunk.

I had a rush of emotions that first night as I entered a new reality as a shelter resident. I was both saddened and fatigued by the situation. I was saddened because eviction was my gateway to homelessness, and I was fatigued from the ongoing struggle to find full-time work and to keep a roof over my head. These were the emotional and mental tolls of spending ninety days sleeping on my brother's couch, seven days at a motel on a charity voucher, and now spending the next thirty days at the shelter. Amazingly, I was hopeful. I knew that the stay was temporary. I was also grateful knowing that I would sooner than later be in position to have my own place, again. As I lay on my bunk, I began to reflect on how I had gotten there. That first night, laying on my bunk, the last thing I remember before falling to sleep was simply asking God, "What is this about?"

The shelter was a four-story brick building located on 5th street, two blocks down from Market Street in downtown Wilmington. Becoming a resident at the shelter would be my first experience living in Wilmington and would be the way that I would first learn about Delaware's largest city. In 2012, Market Street was beginning to experience a renovation as the plans for turning commercial buildings into apartments, the opening of new businesses and restaurants, eventually including a Starbucks, and a new downtown security force with their identifiable yellow shirts and jackets symbolizing a sense of security were underway. Today, Market Street resembles all the money that has been funneled into the area to support entertainment, wining, dining, and living in downtown Wilmington. The transitioning of the downtown area in coming years would bear heavily on people without housing, those identified as homeless not having a presence in the area. This would include banning the selling of *Our Independence*, a newspaper sold by people identifying as homeless to earn income, in the downtown Wilmington area. Wilmington city policies and practices would limit movement of the homeless and that stoked hostilities and raised concerns.

While change was coming to Market Street, around the corner we were surviving at the women's shelter. According to the 2012 Annual Homeless Assessment Report to Congress issued by the U.S. Department of Housing and Urban Development (HUD) there were 633,782 people identified as homeless in the United States. Among that number, 90% of people lived in shelters across ten states, which included Delaware. Counted among Delaware's emergency sheltered homeless were 364 people without children, and 163 families with at least one child. Now, I understand as a shelter resident, I was positioned in that space and at that time to know and connect with some of the human beings counted in that number. Entering the shelter, I would not know how my homeless advocacy would be ignited by what I heard, saw, and could not accept.

Having spent a few days and nights as a resident of the shelter, I found myself becoming more familiar with the expectations for living in a congregate space. Not having the level of privacy I was accustomed to and desired, I found myself adjusting to the energy of other people, meeting curfews, and having to wait my turn to do basic tasks, such as brushing my teeth and taking a shower. I craved alone and down time. Both were elusive living in a homeless shelter. I never experienced a feeling of fear. I can say that there was a feeling of curiosity about the unknown in the space. I had never lived in a congregate setting before. In some way, I believe my curiosity provided me with a sense of calm and helped me focus on seeing how things would unfold as I moved forward.

The last time I had a similar experience was precipitated by the events of September 11, 2001. Traveling home from the U.N. World Conference on Racism in Durban, South Africa, I was among the thousands of people on airplanes flying through Europe redirected to Gander, Newfoundland because we could not enter U.S. airspace. It would be five days before I would reach home. However, unlike so many others, I would eventually reach home to be with family and friends again. I hold a sense of gratefulness, knowing that a twist of fate flying on 9/11 could have made me a fatality. My plane was headed to Washington, D.C.

DeBorah Gilbert White, PhD.

The current situation reminded me of the uncertainty that comes with not knowing those around you, and the forming of a community based on circumstances. Those days spent sleeping on the floor of an elementary school classroom in Gander with strangers was unsettling. I looked at the little chairs and small tables, and the adults detained in the room. We were out of place. I remember feeling like I was on an episode of the television show "Survivor" as a few of the folks in the room had seemingly formed an alliance. They started strategizing about how we could get out of there. They were energized. I was not. I waited to see how each day would unfold, feeling powerless, and simply hoping for the best. Today, I reflect on the limited information, control, and access to resources we had, so where in the hell were we going? Nowhere! However, the situation brought me to a level of understanding vulnerability that spoke to my humanity and the humanity of others in moments of distress. Our plane, along with many others landing in Gander, added over 6,500 people to the population of the town, thereby doubling it. Deplaning, we were instructed to leave our luggage behind. I only had the clothes I was wearing, my pocketbook with my identification, and my non-working cell phone.

A colleague and her partner were on the same flight, so I was not totally with strangers. Having Reverend Sala Nolan and Dr. Diana Gurley with me helped me cope with our current situation. Sala travelled wearing her clerical collar, bringing a certain presence and calm to the situation as a member of the clergy. I remember her being concerned with the wellbeing of the Muslim and Middle Eastern passengers among the group. She spent time engaging and checking in with them. It would be a few more hours before the three of us were able to gather around a television, hear the news reports, and view the images of planes flying into buildings. We stayed together, sleeping next to each other on the classroom floor. It had only been a few days earlier that we were sitting together in a room having an intimate conversation with Archbishop Desmond Tutu as part of a special gathering of a delegation of denominational representatives from the United States. Now, we were being reminded of the extremes of hatred in the loss of and interruption of life.

Over the next few days, I would wait in line to shower, select donated underwear and outer clothing, and obtain food to eat. The second or third day I was able to make a call to family letting them know where I was and that I was relatively okay. There were thousands of us in the same situation, and all we could do was wait. One of the community volunteers befriended Sala, and the three of us were invited to her house to take a less rushed shower, and to have a meal in a less congested atmosphere. She took us to her home, fired up the grill, and along with her husband and two children, provided a lovely meal. We talked about life in the United States, our work with justice issues, and learned about life in Gander over dinner and a bottle of wine. We found a sliver of normalcy in the chaos of the situation by breaking bread together. It was an act of kindness that I will never forget. For a few years after, every September 11th I would reach out to the Gander family, and connect with my other colleagues and sister-friends Carmen Pompey and Reverend Adora Iris Lee traveling from Durban, whose planes were diverted to London, England and Paris, France respectively, to say hello and to reflect on our shared experience of that day.

The evening before leaving Gander, a group of us walked from the school to a neighborhood bar. I decided on having a beer. It was the first time I drank a Samuel Adams, and that night it was the best beer I ever tasted. It continues to be my beer of choice, and always brings back the memory of Gander, and the hospitality of its people. Once home, I listened to my cell messages. Family and friends had reached out to me. It was good to hear their voices. The most heart-breaking and touching message was left by my soon to be sixteen-year-old daughter, Jasmine. Distraught and crying into the phone, she wailed "Mommy, where are you?" The message was left the first day I landed in Gander.

Now, like then, the unknown made me feel vulnerable. I never thought much about shelters until I lived in one. Having lived in one, it was clear to me that although homeless shelters met a need, I understood them to be naturally restrictive and oppressive environments. The culture of the homeless provider services system and shelter environments did little for empowerment. It was simply in the air, some might say a shelter's DNA. There was an element of not feeling secure, and a lack of trust on multiple levels. Each night I slept with my cell phone and laptop tucked close to my body to ensure that they would not go missing. In the mornings when I would shower, I situated my electronics under the covers and placed clothing on top or around them in such a way that would indicate if my bed had been disturbed. Some days I waited for my roommates to leave and would simply close the door to the empty room while across the hall in the bathroom. I never had anything stolen but the possibility had been heightened living in a congregate setting. I found myself adjusting to an environment full of unknowns and having to think and act in different ways.

Residents were required to leave each day, generally after breakfast. While some residents would go to jobs, others may have appointments with potential employers, landlords, or with social services. The children would head off to their schools. A few times, those of us who did not have jobs or appointments to go to were required to participate in a class or workshop facilitated by staff or an outside entity. We would assemble in the dining area which resembled a school cafeteria with its long tables. Instead of benches, we sat on individual chairs. Attendance was required whether the topic was relevant or not. I sat through a presentation on SNAP (Supplemental Nutrition Assistance Program) although I was not eligible. During such times I felt like part of a captive audience, except once. A local bookstore owner and author came to do a writing workshop. Emlyn DeGannes (Ms. Em) of MeJah Books shared a compelling story about her friendship with a young man incarcerated for life and how the letters they exchanged over the years were now compiled in her book *Letters to Ms. Em*. She encouraged us to tap into our creative side, and as a group to think about writing, and possibly doing a writing project together. After the presentation she and I had a short conversation, and she gave me her card. At the time I did not embrace her message. My focus was getting out of the shelter and gaining back the normalcy I once knew for my life. Writing was not on the agenda. However, having Ms. Em's card would prove to be helpful when I began to think about writing about my experience with homelessness. I found her at her bookstore, and we started a friendship that lasts today. She provided early direction for sharing my story and would provide her bookstore as a site for a community event focused on homelessness many years later.

There were opportunities to connect with other residents at breakfast, dinner, or during the weekly rotation of daily shelter chores. I was able to connect to a few of the women over conversation, which uncovered shared interest, and common experiences. Each shelter resident had daily chore assignments that rotated weekly. We primarily worked in teams. One week, I was assigned to bathroom cleaning duty. Like most congregate living situations, people exhibited different levels of cleanliness connected to the maintenance of the body and shared space. I am thankful that I never had to deal with anything too gross, but people could have done better. One week I was assigned to evening cleanup after dinner with a fellow resident, Kim. During our week of wiping down tables, sweeping and mopping the cafeteria floor, I was given snapshots of a woman's life that held so much promise.

DeBorah Gilbert White, PhD.

Kim was a tall, African American woman who wore her hair in braids, which she sometimes wrapped with colorful cloth. Thinking back, I believed one of the reasons we connected was because I often wrapped my head as well. She was an entrepreneur, having once owned a restaurant in another city. Kim was also a survivor of domestic violence at the hands of a husband who had a gambling problem. She relocated to Wilmington, Delaware to get away from him. Her husband's gambling eventually ruined her business, and the beatings nearly broke her spirit. Between the gathering of crumbs with her broom from the cafeteria floor, Kim said, "You will never win married to someone who doesn't respect you and doesn't care about your dreams or aspirations." I stopped wiping tables to look at her and asked, "When did you decide to leave?" She answered, "Too late." At the time, I did not know that Kim was also living with mental health issues. As she swept what she gathered from the floor into the dustpan, I was left without words. However, my thoughts went to how she and I were both at points in our lives to gather the pieces left from our different experiences and to move forward.

During that first week I would periodically look out my room's window, primarily to check on my car. I viewed other residents standing across the street, often with small children in the cold. The mothers would be taking a smoke break. I wondered about the women, the children, and the situation we each now found ourselves in. What were the similarities or differences of the paths that had brought each of us to this point in time? I learned even more about my roommates. Trish was in recovery. She dreaded going to sleep because of the nightmares she had. She slept sitting up, which caused her to breathe loudly when she would fall off to sleep. Trish had awakened next to her boyfriend who had overdosed. She could not get the image of his dead body lying next to her out of her mind. His death was what sent her into recovery. She spent little time in the room, and generally was the first one gone each morning. Diane had been living with family members and no longer had a place to live because they could not get along. She was an adoring grandma (based on how she talked about her grandchild), and at some point had been incarcerated. Brenda, another grandma, had experienced domestic violence. Before the week was over, I knew some part of their stories, and they mine.

I woke one morning to a couple of my roommates complaining about bites. They had been bitten by bedbugs again, and were highly upset. My understanding was that this was an ongoing complaint for my roommates. The shelter management told them that there were no bedbugs. They were basically ignoring the situation. I was not bitten but became disturbed by how the shelter staff and management was choosing to handle the situation. As I sat on my bunk, Diane, highly upset, stood by her bunk, and began showing Brenda and I the bites on her arms and neck. Brenda had also been complaining about bedbug bites. As I listened to the women, I heard their vulnerability, victimization, and disempowerment. Brenda ended her rant with "It shows they don't care. They not even listening to us!" To this I replied, "Get a tissue. They not listening, let's show them." Both women collected the dead bedbugs and took them to the shelter director as evidence.

I left the shelter that day for an appointment with my social worker. I got there early and while sitting in my parked car the thought came to me that more needed to be done about the situation at the shelter. I was angry and acutely sensitive to how not being believed, being ignored, and being dismissed was connected to who you were perceived to be, and the power you were perceived to have. I knew how that translated for me as a child, as a woman, and as an African American. I was now feeling and witnessing it as someone identified as homeless. I called around Wilmington trying to identify who to report the situation to. I believed that there had to be a department of health, or some agency that provided oversight for such matters. I finally did speak with a man who took my information. I have been told it probably was someone at the City of Wilmington's Department of Licenses and Inspections.

Honestly, I cannot remember if it was the same day or the next, but we were moved out of that room. It was quarantined. Whoever came to inspect the premises had cited the shelter for various violations, including bedbugs. After that situation, the shelter director and I had an impromptu conversation where she shared with me all they were doing to eliminate the bedbugs. Although getting rid of the bugs was important, I was still stuck at how the women having the problem had been treated. People who are dealing with the trauma of homelessness do not need to be further traumatized by the people and systems serving them. The situation triggered my own feelings of not having a voice, being made to feel invisible, and feeling like I and my concerns did not matter.

A few days later, another disturbing situation involving our other roommate, Trish, would surface. I learned that she had missed curfew. She showed up past curfew, and the shelter management would not let her in. It was said that Trish was also high, and so she was left out in the cold that February night. I thought that there should be a better way to handle someone who was in relapse, and who in that relapse had broken a shelter rule. There had to be room for compassion, dignity, and humanity. Trish never returned to our room while I was there. I wonder about her; whether she spent the night on the streets or was there a counselor or outreach team she may have connected to.

The women I spent the most time with at the shelter were not my roommates. Some evenings Kim, Rhonda, Michelle, Robin, and I would sit in the common area watching TV and in conversation. It would be during these times that we would touch on the politics of the day, the homeless shelter system, and life in general. Rhonda, another African

American woman, talked often of her involvement with the performing arts, and loss of housing when a relationship ended. Michelle was an African American woman with an eight-year-old daughter. She was polite but guarded. Watching her help her child with homework or engage in their hobby of making jewelry made me wonder about parenting while homeless. I cannot tell you how many children were in the shelter when I was there, but I can tell you that having one there was one too many.

The children ranged from toddlers to school age and were predominantly African American. I never knew why Michelle was at the shelter, but I did buy a bracelet from her. Robin was a thin white woman who was recovering from substance abuse. She was also suicidal, but I did not know that then. She and Rhonda were roommates, and when you saw one, you would often see the other. My relationship with Robin developed through my relationship with Rhonda. The three of us stayed connected through social media after leaving the shelter. A few times Robin would reach out when she was having suicidal thoughts, and I would be among those who would encourage her to connect with her counselor, and to keep choosing life. During one of my last conversations with Rhonda we discussed the possibility of the three of us meeting for lunch or dinner soon.

My first weekend at the shelter started as a gloomy and cold Saturday morning, the date February 11. A significant date for two reasons: it was my fifty-fifth birthday, and later that day I would learn of the death of Whitney Houston (one of my favorite singers). That morning I peered through the blinds to check on my car, parked in its usual spot across the street from the building. I remember thinking of how good it was to have a room with a window facing the street where I could keep an eye on my car and my belongings. That simple fact helped ease some of my anxiety.

DeBorah Gilbert White, PhD.

Shortly, I would be on the road to teach a Saturday class at the University of Phoenix (UOP), Center City campus in Philadelphia. This was a part-time position providing me with a source of income for the last two years. I began exploring teaching shortly after earning my PhD in 2009, to earn money to pay back my student loans. At the time, I was working full time as national staff with the Presbyterian Church (USA) in Louisville, KY. In the Spring of 2010, I became associate faculty with the University of Phoenix teaching online cultural diversity, abnormal psychology, and eventually sociology courses. I was paid by the class, so if I didn't have a class, I didn't get paid. Periodically, I would teach two classes at a time, and on one rare occasion was facilitating three online classes. I found the work rewarding, but unfortunately, as part-time faculty I could never earn enough money to sustain me financially. Now, I was left figuring out how to live without full-time income, and making my periodic part-time income keep me afloat.

It would be later that morning, as I stood before the class, that I experienced a spectrum of emotions. My fifty-fifth birthday had always symbolized a milestone for me. I had envisioned drawing a portion of my pension from the United Church of Christ, an organization I worked with for seventeen years. That money was geared toward making a down payment on a townhouse or condo. This birthday had long represented the turning point to make decisions for a comfortable retirement. Never was turning fifty-five and living in a homeless shelter on my radar. This was a long way from my most memorable birthday when I turned fifty. I had only been working in Louisville for two years and was primarily focused on work and completing my degree. The guy I was dating believed that fifty was too important a birthday to not celebrate in a special way. He convinced me to at least have a quiet dinner with him. I was told to dress up because he had made reservations at a nice restaurant. We arrived at Morton's Steakhouse in downtown Louisville. Entering the restaurant, we were directed to a private room.

He opened the door to a resounding chorus of "Surprise!" Inside were a few of my co-workers. I would learn later that he and my co-worker/friend Roxanna had pulled the event together. Although I nearly fainted, I was pleasantly surprised. It was the best evening. Fast forward five years, I'm standing in a classroom before students trying to focus on teaching while dealing with being homeless and living in a shelter. It did not feel good to be a resident in a women's shelter on any day, and particularly on my birthday. It wasn't supposed to be this way.

During the class break a student returned to the room and shared that Whitney Houston was dead. Many in the classroom including myself, started looking for more information on our cell phones. No one wanted to believe it. Whitney's death spoke to me in the language of gratitude — being grateful for every moment of life, because life was precious and could change as we knew it so quickly. As I reflected on the tragedy of Whitney's death, I was grateful for the joy she had brought to me and thousands of other people with her gift of song. Over the next few days, I found myself viewing and listening to her rendition of "I Love The Lord" from the movie *The Preacher's Wife* on YouTube. Being sheltered homeless, the song ministered to me. I was reminded of my faith, that the current situation would change, that there was hope, and that I was not alone.

My mind was set on leaving the shelter within thirty days. Before entering, I put into motion obtaining a lump sum from my pension. The pension that was set aside to secure my retirement was now the key to my current survival. It would be issued one month after my fifty-fifth birthday. Because of that, I knew in March 2012 my economic situation was going to change for the better. This anticipated happening fueled the hope I maintained, allowing me to endure a most difficult period in my life. The master plan was to get an apartment, and to obtain full-time work in my field. Each

DeBorah Gilbert White, PhD.

week I actively looked for both, and simply thought it would be a matter of time before I would be back on my feet.

Coping

I lived at the shelter for approximately thirty days. It was thirty days where I witnessed some of society's most vulnerable people trying to exist, or coexist, in a most oppressive environment. I was a captive listener to the sharing of life experiences that brought some to this moment. I engaged with women who were in recovery, and the struggle was a daily one. I observed mothers trying to parent children from a sphere of disempowerment, and a reality of displacement that undermined their sense of stability and authority. Kim would sit with me most nights in one of the common areas. As I facilitated my online university class, she would talk about happenings in her room (others would often verify as not true and imaginary), and about a life that had been interrupted by emotional and physical abuse. I would learn that Kim was living with a mental illness. It was clear that she had been traumatized and carried that trauma with her.

I understood trauma to be a person's response to deeply distressing or disturbing life experiences, and that it showed up in different ways for different people. As a social psychologist, I saw clearly how traumatized people could become homeless. Veterans living with post-traumatic stress disorder (PTSD), survivors of physical, emotional, psychological, and sexual abuse, LGBT (lesbian, gay, bisexual, and transgender) youth forced to leave living environments that did not accept who they were and who they loved. I was reminded of the trauma of loss. It showed up for many resulting from the death of family members, divorce, and employment. Experiencing homelessness is traumatic. The situations and circumstances that bring us to homelessness are traumatic. I had my share of trauma. Just maybe Kim sensed the remnants of the trauma I carried.

I would be reminded that we can never know where our help will come from. Kim would be the one who would show me where I could get hot food with my EBT card, take me to a place known as the "Homeless Café" where people experiencing homelessness could go during the day to have a place to "be" without experiencing harassment. It was a space to look at television, bring in food to eat, come in out of the elements, and to simply rest. The "Homeless Café" located in a Wilmington church, was a place of refuge. Kim reminded me that everyone has something they can contribute. Her "street" smarts was a gift to me. My hope was that I provided to her a listening ear, and a knowing that I saw her humanity.

Within walking distance to the shelter was a day center for women called Friendship House. You would enter Friendship House through the bright red side door of the Episcopal Church of Saints Andrew and Matthew and take the steps to the basement. They were known to give out kits with personal care items, such as toothpaste and soap, provide computer time to work on resumes and do job searches, provide bus tickets to access city transportation, and was yet another space for women without housing to congregate. Many of the women from the shelter would frequent this place. Once a month, they offered a group meeting "Ties That Bind" where community people would share information on timely topics, and where an opportunity for women to share in a "safe space" was provided.

I would visit the Ties That Bind group two more times after leaving the shelter: one to sit in on a session, and the next to facilitate a workshop connected to homeless advocacy work I was doing in the community. In the coming years, the Friendship House would combine its outreach serving women and men, end the Ties That Binds group, and change its name to Friendship House Wilmington Empowerment Center. They continue to support people experiencing homelessness, and I remain grateful for how they assisted me.

Most of my days consisted of driving to area libraries or spending many hours at the Wilmington University campus library in New Castle, Delaware on my laptop facilitating my online class. The Wilmington University campus was located a few blocks from the apartment I moved into after leaving Middletown and was evicted from. Each time I passed the street where I once lived, I was reminded of the role it played in where I now found myself.

I had become familiar with the public libraries' hours and days of operation to have other places to go away from the shelter. On some days, I was looking at apartments, as I took steps toward the day that I would be in my own place. As my time got closer to leaving the shelter, my observations and conversations with fellow residents focused more on systemic issues. I began to wonder why the images and narratives connected to homelessness did not focus more on the growing number of women and children who were identified as homeless?

I often thought about how the stereotypes about homelessness and who was homeless did not tell the full story. I began to reflect on how I was made to feel inside and outside the shelter as someone identified as homeless. I thought about writing a research paper to assist in removing the stigma, and the heavy focus on individual causation, and bring more focus to the systemic and structural considerations for the experience of homelessness, and overall poverty in a country of abundance. I remember thinking about the patient and airline passenger bills of rights. I wondered about having a similar document for those who were experiencing homelessness. Each day surviving, observing the women and children, and learning about homelessness weighed heavily on my awareness of the disparities and injustices of society. It also provided me with an even deeper realization of the power of story or narrative, and how narrative framed realities. I fell in love with narrative and personal story researching, and writing my dissertation. Everyone has a story, or stories. Listening to the stories of others, and reflecting on my own life's highs and lows, twists and turns, in my state of homelessness prompted me to want to share mine. The question I asked God the first night in the shelter, "What is this about?" was slowly being answered. I now realize it was about change.

Underemployed and Evicted

In the Spring of 2010, I became unemployed after working five years as national staff with the Presbyterian Church (USA) in Louisville, KY. As part of the organization's downsizing, I received a severance package that included employment outplacement services. Without the option to apply for unemployment, and with limited employment opportunities in Kentucky, I decided to return East (I'm a native New Yorker) to seek better employment opportunities, and to be closer to family and friends. I was now faced with starting over in my fifties, knowing that there was still much I could contribute to the workplace.

The state of Delaware would become my new home. It was centrally located to the New York City, Philadelphia, Baltimore, and Washington, D.C. job markets, the cost of living was cheaper, and I had one relative currently living there — my brother, Jeffrey. September 2010, we loaded my car and a UHAUL (driven by my brother) and along with my two cats, headed to Delaware. I would spend the latter part of 2010 and early 2011 in a place called Middletown, Delaware. Middletown at that time was what many would describe as a bedroom community. It was quiet. It was slow paced and supported images I held about small town USA. I never lived in a place that had such a small business or commercial area, and no hospital. It would be here that I would meet my first new friend in Delaware, Renee, who lived in the house across the street. She was a New York transplant and taught at Middletown High. Our conversations were always interesting, especially when sharing New York memories and educator stories.

DeBorah Gilbert White, PhD.

I continued to teach for the University of Phoenix online while collecting severance pay and seeking full-time employment after the move to Delaware. I was underemployed. I was looking for work that would provide income and benefits comparable to my last employer. The last ten years working as national staff for two religious denominations afforded me a middle-class lifestyle that allowed me to not have any concerns meeting my basic needs. In 2010, between my full-time and part-time income, I was making more than $70,000 a year, with great healthcare benefits. My education and experience prepared me for a leadership position as a diversity and inclusion specialist, chief diversity officer, and for organizational change and development work. At the very point that I envisioned my degree working for me in a way that would boost my finances, it felt like life events had me on another track. Not being able to secure a full-time position that would pay me for my experience and knowledge was disappointing and life changing. I ended my stay in Middletown, and in March 2011 moved to a city called New Castle, Delaware. New Castle had more of a city feel, and was located right outside of Wilmington, Delaware's largest city. I was still seeking full-time employment and was struggling due to my limited income. Unfortunately, another reality was looming over the horizon. My monetary resource options were dwindling with the severance package nearing its end. Finding work had become more critical than ever.

This experience looking for work would be different from what I remembered from my earlier work searches. After all, it had been seventeen years since I truly looked for work. No longer were there phone inquiries or walking into a business and asking for an application. It was a different world with everything being done online. There was also the reality that the last two organizational positions I held were the result of applying for a program management position at an organization I worked with for over twelve years, and being recruited to apply for a newly created position at the other. I was entering uncharted waters.

The span of my job search included applications for teaching positions at Delaware universities. I also applied for the position of Special Assistant at the Institute for Children, Poverty, and Homelessness, and Director of Employment and Education at Lantern Community Services, both in New York. I applied for the Diversity Program Specialist position at the U.S. Department of Health and Human Services in D.C., and for the National Consumer Advocate position at Health Care for the Homeless Inc. in Baltimore. I registered with Christiana Care Health System in Delaware. My application to Stand By Me Delaware resulted in a team interview, but no job.

At one point I thought ageism may have been a factor; I could not get an interview to save my life! I experienced most places not responding at all, however, I got a few "nice" rejection letters. Not being able to obtain full time employment over an extended period of time has a toll. I began to reflect on what the universe might be telling me. Maybe, I wasn't supposed to be looking to work for anyone. Was I to fully pursue a consulting career? I didn't know. However, I was able to remain hopeful when I changed my perspective from looking for a job to securing income and having multiple streams of it. The experience of being downsized taught me the need for multiple streams of income. In the coming years, I was able to have streams of income that satisfied meeting my basic needs, without having a full-time job. It was an answered prayer.

I was running out of money. I needed to keep my cell phone on. I needed to keep my electricity on. I needed to have food to eat. I needed to stay housed. The severance ended and the struggle was real. My part-time salary from teaching was not enough. I was slipping into another type of existence, that of the working poor. I began to make calls to former colleagues and friends. I asked them for at least twenty-five dollars to help me keep my cell phone and electricity on. This would be presented as a loan request, with promise of payment as the monies from teaching came in. My sister-friend, and former colleague at the Presbyterian Church (USA) Roxanna, came through. Another former colleague, Belinda, sent me a check. Both of their actions prevented the lights in the apartment and cell phone from being shut off. Roxanna would help me a few more times by using her credit card to pay something on my phone bill when my phone service was in jeopardy. This allowed me to stay connected with potential employers, my family, and the students I taught. These women really did not know the lifeline their generous acts would be.

My mom, who was living in another state, sent money to pay my rent. I did not want to take it. Every reason I gave for her not to do it, she provided another reason why to do it. Finally, she simply said, "It's what family does," and so, I accepted the gesture. This was a turning point for me in how I looked at accepting assistance or help from others. People would tell me "not to block their blessing" and as a person of faith, I understood the desire to be a blessing to others. However, it was such an uneasy feeling to have your senior citizen, retired parent sending you money, while understanding she was living on a fixed income. I learned later that she got the money to help me from her retirement annuity. Hearing about the pending loss of my apartment, and my becoming homeless, my mom imagined me living on the streets. Like many others, she viewed homelessness only as people on the street. My mom expressed that she was shocked when I lost my apartment and became homeless. I guess like me, she thought I would be able to get a job with my credentials, or at least the social services needed. She shared that she felt the family had failed me.

Mom knew of my struggle because my brother visited me and noticed that my cupboards and refrigerator were not full. He reported back to her that I didn't have any food. I was furious to tears. The truth was, I didn't have much, but I was not facing starvation. I didn't have what I would have liked to have, but I had not missed a meal. The truth was living alone, I never had a refrigerator filled with food. I did a lot of eating out and carry out, and not too much cooking. In later weeks, my brother and I would explore the possibility of moving in together. The thinking was for him to be placed on my lease, and we would pool our money together to pay the bills. This temporary arrangement would be until the end of my current lease that was ending in early 2012. I would avoid eviction, and he would have fewer housing expenses. For some reason we were not able to implement that plan, and I continued to struggle. Again, it was a reminder of being in a perfect storm; that place where it seemed that nothing was going right, and it seemed inevitable that it was not going to get any better soon. I saw the storm coming and I could not avoid it.

I intentionally did not tell my young adult children. I did not want them to worry about or feel responsible for me. I do not know if their knowledge of the situation would have made a difference in keeping the apartment. My son, Malcolm, lived in Cincinnati, OH. He moved there years earlier to attend the University of Cincinnati and stayed. He was dealing with living and working as a young African American man, in a city that was having its share of racial issues. Our conversations at the time, focused often on him being racially profiled, and his sharing frustrations about the police shootings, and the escalating violence in our communities. We would often have these conversations as he walked home from work late at night. I felt that he had a sense of security having me on the phone as he navigated the streets to his apartment.

Like many African American mothers, I knew the resulting fear and dread of my son having an encounter with police. Again, I did not want to be a distraction, thinking that I would find a way out of my own situation. Years later, he would share with me that learning about my experience of homelessness shocked and saddened him. He never thought about one of his parents or someone with a degree being homeless. The image he held was someone on the streets, mentally ill, or an alcoholic. Knowing that his mom was not on the streets, was not mentally ill, or an alcoholic, yet became homeless helped him move beyond those stereotypes. When I asked his feelings about me sharing my story, he told me, "You could never go wrong being real."

My daughter, Jasmine, was on her first assignment as a U.S. Foreign Service Officer working out of the country, living in Ethiopia. She was on assignment for two years working across the continent of Africa with the African Union. I did not want to have anything be a distraction to her first career assignment with the U.S. Department of State. She could not remember how she became aware of my homelessness, but felt embarrassed for herself in that she questioned, "How did I not know?" Jasmine shared that it weighed heavily with her what people would think about her having a mom who experienced homelessness during a time that she was living well, making good money, and could have helped. She did not understand why I did not tell her.

During our last conversation on the matter, I was reminded how both she and Malcolm had helped pay my cell bill a few times, and she had also gifted me money from time to time. All the money that came my way during the time I was struggling to keep housing, helped me to hold on as long as I did. My mothering instinct was to be protective of them both by not being a burden. Years later, I would consider if pride was part of the equation in how I chose to handle the situation with my children. I would lean more toward a mixture of embarrassment and fear. I was feeling the embarrassment of being in a situation that my life accomplishments said I should not be in. There was fear of being a distraction, and fear of having failed them.

Neither one of them needed to carry the weight of what their mother was going through. I do not know if they had any awareness of my homelessness, while I was experiencing it. I do know that I didn't tell. When I asked Jasmine her thoughts about my experience she said "I'm proud of your perseverance, and ability to find strength out of struggle. You seem to have found your path. Becoming homeless was a different way to figure it out, but you have been able to find your purpose. That is my prayer, that I find mine." As I reflected on what my children shared, I was reminded of feeling like I was on a runaway train, nothing I did seemed to stop the inevitable. I'm not sure if telling them would have stopped my experiencing homelessness, or simply would have delayed it. On some level, I believe that going through the experience was a necessary means to an end. I was now equipped to address the need for transformative change better than I could before.

Weeks before the eviction, I shared my situation with a friend and fellow church member Rose. She trusted me enough to share that she was experiencing housing insecurity and shared that the church could possibly help me. They helped her. This was hopeful and I followed up with the information she provided. I applied for financial assistance from the church I belonged to, New Destiny Fellowship. After going through the process, one of the church trustees met me at the rental office of my apartment complex and the church paid $500.00 toward my rent. I was directed by someone in the community to also connect with a Catholic Church that was around the corner from where I lived. I called Our Lady of Fatima Catholic Church and shared that I needed help paying my rent, and that I was facing eviction. I was told that such requests were responded to based on a special offering the church lifted on Sundays. That Monday, I got a call that they would assist me. The management office called a few days later letting me know that there were people there wanting to make a payment toward my rent. I went to the office, met, and thanked them. I do not remember how much they paid, but I do remember being grateful. I would later send them a thank you note.

After going through savings, asking family, friends, and my church for help, I was still left wondering, how was I going to pay my bills, particularly my rent with inadequate income. In my desperation, I applied for social services. Unfortunately, I could not check any of the boxes that would qualify me to receive assistance. I was not pregnant. I was not living with an addiction, mental illness, or physical disability. I did not have small children. I was not caring for someone who was elderly and dependent on me. I was out of luck. I reached out to Samaritan Outreach, a community organization that among other services, provided vouchers to local food pantries. It was a way I would be able to supplement my dwindling food budget. The connection to Samaritan Outreach was the beginning of my community exposure to poverty, hunger, and homelessness in Delaware. They were part of an organization called the Ministry of Caring which also operated two dining rooms in Wilmington, and a clothing closet and facilities for people to take showers at the location I visited. It was here that I first shared space with people experiencing street homelessness as they sought services. It was a busy place.

One day, I received a call from a case manager at Samaritan Outreach. A local news outlet was doing a story on the changing face of poverty and homelessness in Delaware. The reporter would be coming to their office and she thought he should hear my story. This would be the first of three interviews with Jon Hurdle, a reporter with WDDE, Delaware's National Public Radio (NPR) affiliate. That first story "Delaware Feels the Pain of Rising Poverty" ran in October 2011. I would be identified as homeless in November. The conversations with Jon would serve to document my experience before homelessness, after exiting shelter homelessness, and my advocacy journey for homeless legislation in the state of Delaware.

The struggle to keep housing was ongoing. I would continue to make payments toward the rent, as my income allowed. I was living in a fog, overwhelmed by the stress of the situation. I was consistently late, and consistently owing. My eviction process had begun August, 2011. Delaware Justice of the Peace Court 13, case #JP13-11-011992 had been filed. I was being evicted for owing $623.00 for rent. My monthly rent was $599.00. In retrospect that does not seem like a lot of money. However, it was more than I had access to at the time. What I did not know was that people in Delaware, like many other places across the country, were experiencing high eviction rates. Delaware at one point would come to be identified as one of the states in the U.S. with the highest number of evictions. I came to understand that someone could be evicted in Delaware for owing less than five dollars. It was problematic for me that such a small amount of money could facilitate homelessness. It was clear that stopping evictions was key to homeless prevention.

I was underemployed. My part-time employment income was not steady due to periodically not having a class to teach. I knew that I did not have the income to maintain the apartment. Understanding that there was no homeless preventive aid to help me, I accepted as fact that I would lose housing. The constant struggle to make ends meet had taken its toll. I had no fight left in me. In hindsight, I believe that if I had at least ninety days of rental assistance, I could have held on to my place, knowing that I could pull my pension in March 2012. In retrospect, I'm left wondering who would have paid my rent until March when I would draw my pension. At the time, I could not identify a soul. The housing court date was October 3, 2011. It was the beginning of a journey that would set me emotionally, psychologically, and spiritually on a path that I would have never imagined. I remember the anxiety I felt anticipating that I would come home and find eviction papers posted on my front door. I had always felt disturbed when I saw such papers on the doors of others. I viewed it as degrading and shaming behavior. There were only four units in my building, and I only knew my neighbors in passing. We barely saw each other. My apartment was on the first floor of the building, so everyone entering or leaving the building would know that I had not paid my rent. They would also know that I was being thrown out. I felt shame about them possibly knowing that I was being evicted. According to the Eviction Lab at Princeton University, there were 19,174 evictions filed, and 6,686 people evicted in Delaware in 2011. I was in that number.

Years later, I would be asked if I thought the eviction was an illegal eviction. The only answer I had was "I owed the money." There was nothing available within the court system or social services at that time to help save my housing. At the time of the eviction, I was in survival mode, and the thought never crossed my mind to seek counsel, nor was it suggested by any of the agencies I connected with. Today, we know that many housing advocates are pushing for the Right to Counsel for individuals and families facing eviction. We know that Right to Counsel can prevent homelessness.

I do think having counsel would have made a difference connected to actions taken or not taken after the hearing. Years after my eviction, I called the courts to verify the date the judgment connected to my eviction was satisfied. I was told that the judgment was still standing. I lost my breath. Although I had paid my former landlord all back rent and court fees in 2012, they never did their part to inform the court! My former landlord was apologetic about not informing the court and ensured me that they would. A follow up call to the court a few months later informed me that the judgment was finally showing satisfaction on April 22, 2019. I will never know the impact this oversight had on my credit report, housing, or employment options. I do know it did not help. This incident raises the broader consideration regarding the ask for legal representation and the right to counsel that is building momentum across the nation connected to landlord and tenant issues. I'm thinking that if I had counsel, that oversight would not have happened.

In the coming weeks, I started preparing to give up the apartment. I began to downsize. It seemed that no matter what I did, I could not stop the inevitable. I was going to lose my housing. Although I had reached out to family, friends, and my church, and had cut my living expenses by frequenting food pantries, not subscribing to cable, and not participating in social activities involving money (there was no disposable income), I did not have enough income to meet my most basic needs. I prepared for what was to come as best I could. What had not been discarded, sold, given away, or put into storage, was packed in a few boxes and two suitcases. The boxes consisted of my most important personal documents, books, teaching materials, and personal care items. The suitcases held seasonal clothing. All would be placed in my car.

At the time, I never thought about people living in their cars. It was not something that even crossed my mind regarding myself in the present situation. The reality for me would not be to live in a car, or to be someone who would need to find a place to rest or sleep in any of the other uninhabitable spaces and places people without housing could find themselves. My reality would be to not have stable, safe, secure housing, and to know what it truly felt like to not have a place to call home. I remember at one point, during my experience with homelessness yearning to have a key, to place in a door, to the space I called home. Over the years I have come to recognize that having housing is foundational to all other matters of life. Not only does housing provide protection from the elements, but it also serves to be a place to retreat mentally, to rest physically, and a place to express your individuality. Having a permanent address demonstrated stability, responsibility, and being part of a community, as an adult home usually represented a peaceful space, and a place where I nurtured myself. Being identified as homeless challenged the ability to do that.

I asked one friend from church, Carolyn, to care for my plants. I also gifted her my desk and hutch. My friends Lori and Delores let me store some items and boxes in their garages. During one of my visits with Lori, she gifted me a jar of coins, explaining that she didn't know how much money was in the jar, but it was mine. After converting the coins to bills, I called Lori to thank her for her generosity. There was over $30.00 in the jar, and it helped me immensely.

I placed ads on Craigslist selling my larger furniture pieces, including a bookcase and daybed. My friend Sherri showed up to be with me as strangers answering the ads came to view and buy items. Preparing for eviction involved giving away pieces of my life. It represented loss. These material items were connected to personal and professional memories. They were some of the tangibles showing where I had been and what I had done. It was comforting to know that I had women around me that supported me in the ways that I needed. It would be that awareness and understanding of sisterhood, and the importance of genuine female relationships that would lay the foundation for my future work connected to the issue of homelessness.

On November 3, 2011, the Constable posted the eviction notice on my apartment door. I called Jeffrey and asked if I could stay with him. When I shared with him that my two cats would be with me, he became less receptive. Yet, he opened his apartment to the three of us. We really had no other place to go. We were homeless. My two cats (sister and brother rescues as kittens) and I stayed with my brother in his one-bedroom apartment. His convertible couch would be where I would lay my head for approximately the next three months. I often referred to Jeffery as my baby brother. There is a two-year difference between us. He had a helpful spirit, and I appreciated that about him. Jeffrey was a commercial bus driver. Over his career he worked for a major national bus line, municipal bus lines, private companies, and as a school bus driver. Our schedules were different, which made our cohabitation work. Depending on his work schedule, he could leave early in the morning before the crack of dawn, or be gone for a few days.

It was while staying with Jeffrey that I applied again for assistance from social services. My eviction had opened the door for me to receive an EBT card for food, Medicaid, and a small monthly check. Also, I began to teach on campus for the University of Phoenix Center City location in Philadelphia, PA. This would provide another opportunity to obtain additional income, although part time. The realization that a few months earlier, I contacted social services to prevent the eviction, and now, identified as homeless, I finally received some help, troubled me. As a healthy, single, capable female with housing, who simply did not have enough income, social services could not help me, or direct me to someone that could. I remember thinking that the system was not set up for people like me. The system had been set up to be reactive rather than proactive. Its goal was to aid society's most vulnerable. However, my potential loss of housing did not make me vulnerable enough. It was sobering.

It felt like people like me, those who could not check the boxes, were left to fall through the cracks, and I did. All I can say is that every encounter I had trying to obtain services was tainted with frustration. It generally started with the forms, and always having to declare whether I was addicted, not recently released from jail or a mental facility, or pregnant. The system functions were framed by a stereotypical and limited lens of its clients. That disturbed me. There were new "faces of homelessness" and the system was not reflective of, or prepared for that.

Two years later, I would stand before Delaware Legislators in the state capital, sharing my experience and asking "Why, as a citizen of the state, I could not get help to keep housing?" This question would become more pertinent with a growing and changing homeless problem, and with a lack of beds in Delaware shelters to address the problem. I thought it was a fair question. Through the lens of homelessness, I began to understand the vicious cycle of poverty and how it was supported by social stigma, and those social structures and systems that seemed more focused on managing homelessness, rather than ending it. I also understood that I truly represented the changing face of homelessness, and the need to expand the narrative related to it. I continued to hold on to hope that my circumstances would change. I believed that it was just a matter of time that one of the places I applied for full-time work would call me in for an interview.

The stay with my brother would be more temporary than I thought. His lease was up in the early new year, and he was not going to renew. I decided to pull my pension and began completing the paperwork. A ray of hope would be eventually having money to support having my own housing again. I was in that in-between time, where you are coming out of a difficult situation, immersed in uncertainty, but knowing that change was just over the horizon. Having secured state assistance, the case manager with social services was now assisting me with finding another place to live. He was looking at shelters.

I was referred to the West End Neighborhood House. West End offered a program that assisted families with becoming more self-sufficient. It was here I met my case manager, Karen Summa, who would emerge as an angel on my path. We met periodically to explore options, and to create and discuss a budget. Like many people experiencing homelessness, my issue was not lack of budgeting skills, but a lack of income. After sharing that I would shortly need to leave my brother's place, she secured a voucher from Martha's House, a church resource that provided transitional housing for women experiencing homelessness. Toward the end of January 2012, my cats and I would find ourselves as residents of a local motel for one week. That voucher would be used to cover my stay at the motel. During my last visit we talked about my waiting for a bed to open at a shelter and what to do with my cats once that happened.

I had been trying to figure out a way to keep my cats safe, and preferably with me. In private moments, I felt overwhelmed by the uncertainty of finding a place for them and myself. I remember thinking "I have lost nearly everything. I can't lose them." It began to feel as if I needed to hold on to them to prove to myself that I could manage the situation, and that I was still a responsible person. Karen offered to take my cats in until I could secure permanent housing. I decided to take her up on her offer, but only after a bed had been located at a shelter. Years later, I asked her why she had shown such generosity to me. She explained that she sensed how stressed I was about their care, that she understood the bond between people and their pets, and that having a pet friendly home, it simply made sense for her to offer. I was thankful. It was another lesson in not knowing from where or from whom your help would come.

Because I had to sneak the cats into the motel, I did not allow anyone into the room, not even to clean. I set up what the cats needed in the bathroom, and did the room upkeep myself. I would have housekeeping simply leave fresh washcloths and towels. One of my cats liked windows, so I did my best to block the windows with items so that she would not find her way on the other side of the curtains. But she did, and that made me fearful that we might get thrown out. The room was located on the side of the motel facing a busy street. Much of the traffic could be attributed to cars coming off the Delaware Bridge. I can't express the terror I felt returning to the room one afternoon, to find her sunning in the window without a care in the world. There she was, stretched out, as if everything was fine. Not knowing how long she had been in the window, and if motel management was aware of her, I waited nervously for a knock on the door. My cats and I were in a continuous survival mode. It had been that way for some time. I was not one to break rules for the sake of breaking rules; however at this point, rules were broken twice related to my pets in my desperation. That reality reminded me to not say what you would never do. It also helped me to release judgment about people's actions in desperate situations.

Transitions

Losing employment and housing are life transitions that too many people can relate to. The loss of income or lack of a living wage is often foundational to individuals and families having the capacity to maintain housing. The recent global pandemic has provided a reality check about vulnerability. It is often said that many of us are a paycheck away from the struggle to meet the basic needs of maintaining housing, having enough food to eat, and proper clothing. Why we are made vulnerable and how we, as individuals and a society, respond to that vulnerability makes a difference. My vulnerability did not start with losing full-time income or housing. I now know that I had been navigating being vulnerable all my life.

My first recollection of a major life transition was my three siblings and I going to live with our paternal grandmother and her husband in the Bronx. Their one-bedroom apartment was on Sherman Avenue, off 167th Street near the Grand Concourse. We had moved from the projects to living in an apartment building. There were less people around us, and there was no real play area. We would no longer be bussed to school, but simply walk down the block and cross the street to go to school that year. I remember a pizza shop located on 167th street (a busy and wide street with cars moving in both directions) that we would walk to regularly. I have memories of sitting on the step outside of the apartment building eating Italian Ice on many hot summer days and evenings. For some reason, I don't hold any memories about living in that apartment. Now, I think I was simply trying to figure out what was going on. I have two pictures of my dad in the apartment, at what seems to be a birthday celebration. In one, he is sitting at the kitchen table taking a bite out of a slice of birthday cake held in his hands, and in the other he is sitting in front of his birthday cake surrounded by his four children. We are all smiling and seemingly happy. I don't remember the day. Thank God for pictures.

I came to understand that my dad lived with a mental illness called paranoid schizophrenia, and he had become threatening and physically abusive to my mom. As his mental health declined, his behaviors were more irrational and unpredictable. The issuing of a protective order, and the possible loss of custody to the state weighed heavily in Mom's decision to have us live with Nana. We went from being with our mom and dad, to seeing our mom at least once a week, and not seeing our dad at all. My father suffered a "nervous breakdown" and was hospitalized. At the time we were told nothing, and I learned from the silence surrounding my dad growing up, that a "nervous breakdown" was something, and he was someone to be afraid of and to feel ashamed about. None of the adults in my life demonstrated they were aware or understood the emotional cost to me or my siblings. Today, I recognize my siblings and I had experienced displacement due to mental illness and domestic violence, and nobody said a word to us. Dad and mental illness were made invisible through silence. It was the 1960's and the start of my secret keeping.

I was seven and the oldest. We were considered stair steps with my sister Cassandra age 6, brother Jeffrey age 5, and sister Theodora nearly one. We were living in the East River Housing Projects: 440 E. 105th Street, in Manhattan, New York to be exact. I remember the pride I felt as a kid in knowing and reciting my address to anyone who would listen, the fun playing with other kids in the project's play areas, and the love of my paternal great grandmother, Irene

Miller, who we knew as Mama I. We lived in the same building as Mama I, she on the 8th floor, and we on the 9th floor. Dad, Mom, Cassandra, Jeffrey, and I all lived with her before getting our own place. I remember our apartment having a large fish tank with goldfish and hanging glass chimes shaped in rectangles with bright color spots that made the most beautiful sound to my little ears. Watching the fish and hearing the chimes often mesmerized me.

I remember my mother dressing my sister and I like twins (we were ten months apart), Buster Brown shoes, and me wearing those pink and blue girl cat eyeglasses, which I hated. More than once I "lost" them by throwing them away. We did many things as a family, like picnics on Wards Island which was walking distance across a bridge near the projects, taking Easter pictures with the East River as a backdrop, and often attending Metropolitan Baptist Church in Harlem, where Mama I sang in the choir and belonged to a few of the church's auxiliaries. I remember our dad singing "Only God Can Make A Tree" and making us laugh with his theatrics. A conversation with Jeffrey reminded me of Dad's love of playing chess, and basketball as well.

I remember us as kids sitting on the couch in the living room at night with only the light from the television watching "Peyton Place" with Mom. I also remember jumping around to the sound of Miriam Makeba singing "Pata Pata" and liking her voice and the music. My parents loved her, and I believe she was the first artist from Africa that I had an awareness of. She was my first connection to the motherland, and every time I hear that song, even now, I experience happiness. I also remember doing "The Twist" dancing and laughing so hard until it hurt. Chubby Checker's popular song and dance represented fun. One of my favorite things was hearing the jingle of the Mister Softee Ice Cream truck and running to meet it with Cassandra and Jeffrey. Up until seven years old, I enjoyed the innocence of childhood and the joy of family.

We often hear about girls missing their dads. I have come to realize that I was a girl who missed not only the bonding and love of a father in my life, but also a girl missing connection with a mom in a way that met my emotional needs. At seven, you don't have the words or skill to express all that you feel. You don't understand, but you know when something is different. Both parents worked. Dad passed the written test to become a New York City Corrections Officer but failed the psychological portion. It was an indication of things to come. Mom worked a split shift with AT&T and would later work for and retire from the U.S. Postal Service.

In retrospect, he was sick and absent. She was present, traumatized, and overwhelmed. They both were young with four little children. Perhaps, too much too soon. This is not a criticism. It is an observation as an adult. It was a setup for developing both daddy and mommy issues connected to trust and abandonment, for me. I have often reflected on my mom's decision as one that did allow my siblings and I to stay together. Mom shared how during one of her court appearances to obtain a restraining order, the judge suggested that if the home environment was not safe for her children, the New York City foster care system would be the answer. Placing us in the care of Nana diverted us from possibly being separated. Mom remained involved in our lives and continued to provide for us.

Although we lived with our paternal grandmother, we had relationships with our aunts, uncles, cousins, and maternal grandmother, Alma. I hold fond memories of spending summer days with my mom's side of the family: great grandma Roof (who as a child, I mistakenly called and knew as grandma Ruth, thinking that we were calling her by her first name, rather than her last. Her first name was Alice), and other extended family in the outskirts of Egg Harbor, NJ. I have always felt blessed to have known my grandmothers and great grandmothers. I never knew my dad's father and had a distant relationship with my mom's dad. They both were named Willie. My familial interactions taught me that relationships are built, and family was more than those we held blood ties to. Sometimes family was made with those we crossed paths with on life's journey. That was true for me.

There were a few occasions in subsequent years that we would see Dad, but he was not really a part of our lives. As a young adult, and even now, it hurts me to think what he was possibly thinking, if at all, about the lack of relationship he had with his children. There was no blame or anger toward him on my part. I simply wondered if he knew he was loved. This persistent thought drove me to look for him many years later. I only had two interactions with my dad as an adult. The first was after finding him, and visiting where he was staying, in single room occupancy housing, after New York had moved from institutional to a community care model for people living with mental illness. He was happy to see me, and we had polite conversation as I updated him on myself, siblings, and shared a few pictures. I informed him he was a grandfather of two. At the time, his daughters, Cassandra and Theodora, were mom to one child each. The second would be sharing one dinner together with my boyfriend at our Queens, New York apartment. Dad was quiet, but he had shown up.

A few weeks passed after the dinner, and I could not reach him by phone. I went to where he was living only to find out that he was dead. Cause of death: cirrhosis of the liver. I'm left wondering if he knew how ill he was when we last saw each other. I was told that he had been dead in his room for some time. It was summertime. The contamination from his decomposing body made it impossible to retrieve any of his belongings. There is nothing that I have materially that I can say was my father's. I was informed to contact the New York City Coroner's office because his body was probably already headed to Potter's Field, the place where unclaimed bodies were buried in mass graves. Thankfully, his body was still at the city morgue and I was asked to come in and identify him. It was one of the most difficult things I ever had to do. I stood at a glass window, while my dad's decomposed body was presented, and the only thing that reminded me of him was the shape of his head and his teeth. I stood there as a twenty-six-year-old in age, but a seven-year-old in my heart. I couldn't stop crying. I believe the tears were for what would never be, what had been lost, and for all the unknown possibilities. Nana went into denial. She questioned and challenged whether I had identified the right person. She did not believe it was him. Mom was out of the country on vacation when I shared the news with her. She paid for the funeral. They never divorced, and although separated for many years, she maintained a life insurance policy on him. Many of the questions I had for him would be left unanswered, buried in the ground with him, and in my mind. Dad was buried Labor Day weekend. That weekend has never been the same for me since then.

Being a parent myself, I don't think that any of us are fully prepared for all that parenthood entails. Neither one of my parents were prepared for the challenges they encountered. I also think about my grandmother, Nana, carrying her fear, guilt, and shame about her only child, yet she took us in. Nana worked as a domestic, door to door salesperson, and a senior caregiver across her life. She was a teenage unwed mother when she, my dad, and Mama I migrated to New York City from Ocala, Florida in the 1930's. She carried with her much social stigma. Dad's mental illness ensured that stigma remained alive and well in our family.

Three other definitive transitions would round out the shaping of my life. They were marriage, parenthood, and divorce. I met Granville White while working for a company selling children's educational materials and other items over the phone. We were telemarketers. I noticed him talking with another co-worker, Delrena, who became a work friend of mine. Any shifts we worked together, he would find a way to talk to me, and it would end up with him always asking me out. I checked him off as a "playa." One day, Delrena said to me "You know, he really likes you." To which I responded, "No girl, he's always talking to you!" She answered, "Yes, about you!" We were opposites. He was loud, he smoked, and it was annoying how he would always "pop" up. I was cordial and remained uninterested.

As the workplace friendships developed, I would discover that he was funny, we held somewhat similar political views, and he was a good guy. Delrena, Granville, and another work friend, Charlie, would hang out from time to time. Granville persisted, and we had our first date. We went to Sammy's, a popular seafood restaurant on City Island in the Bronx. I was twenty-five years old; it was the second date I had ever been on, and the first time I would eat lobster tail. It continues to be a favorite seafood choice.

At the time, I was caught up in an emotionally and sexually abusive situation. I wasn't looking for a relationship, but I was looking for a way out. It had been that way since I was around eleven years old, and sometimes I think before then, when I had flashbacks of earlier childhood bath sessions that ended with discomfort between my legs. I had been groomed well. I didn't tell when it happened. I attribute this to fear, confusion, and not trusting the adults in my life to protect me. After all, it was one of them hurting me. Today, I would say that my step grandfather was a pedophile. He was also a minister, and eventually a pastor. He tried to get me to bring a neighbor playmate to him. We will never know how many children he violated. He told me that God had given me to him. There was no way I could fight God. I was conditioned to fear God. Once I began to understand how he manipulated me as a child, teen, and into young adulthood, I realized all that was taken that I could never get back. I hated him for robbing me of my innocence. In later years, I connected my feelings, and responded strongly to any situation that reeked of me not having a choice, being made to feel powerless, devalued, or dishonored. Each was a trigger for my trauma. I was angry with him, and in some ways with myself. It haunted me that I stayed in the situation for so many years. I believe, on some level I checked out, numbing myself to the situation, and that kept me somewhat sane. Second guessing myself was a weight that I needed to drop to move forward from shame and guilt.

My emotional development was arrested at seven years old. It was further compromised by my pre-teens. I now understand that I was emotionally bankrupt and numbed by two traumatic childhood experiences. I didn't have power, and I didn't have a voice. At the time, I did not know that I was participating in self-harm by periodically pulling out strands of my hair. I now know that was a response to my trauma. I was told by my abuser that nobody would believe me. I believed him. I felt distant from my grandmother and my mom. I couldn't tell them. The space had not been created for me to say, "Nana, or Mommy, he's hurting me." Unfortunately, years later, when his deeds came to light, neither one of them handled it properly. I have come to reconcile the situation as one where they both did the best they could at the time. I had to.

Despite what I was experiencing, I was an excellent student in school, never abused drugs, participated in church piano recitals and choirs, and wasn't sexually promiscuous, but often felt socially awkward. I was a highly functioning mess. Over the years, I have pondered why I didn't stick a needle in my arm, find a corner to work, or become someone's cell mate. Growing up in the Missionary Baptist Church tradition, I thought I didn't have a testimony because I had not been delivered from anything like the aforementioned. I was in an emotional hell that no one seemed to see. I knew too much too soon, my feeling of safety was eroded, and my sense of trust was destroyed. I learned to carry secrets early in life and learned to be afraid of what people might think about me if they knew. I lived my family's pathology of silence. I kept the secrets at all costs.

My friendship with Delrena allowed me to gradually open up to her. She was the big sister I never had. One day I told her what was going on with me. My friends at work came through for me. Delrena helped me pack my things and I moved in with Granville to figure out my next steps. I talked them out of bringing harm to my abuser, not for his sake, but for my grandmother's. They shared with me what they could do. I know I saved his life. I was out of that situation, and he was not worth any of us doing jail time. Coming out of that situation I saw myself as a survivor. My thinking was that the best revenge would be to live my life with purpose, and to live it well. I would not let family history or dynamics destroy the future.

It would be years before I would share any portions of the experience, and only if I thought it would help the person I was sharing it with in some way. Not accepting victimhood was key to not only living my life, but to thrive. I was delayed and sidetracked in many ways, but I was not destroyed. Granville and I were living together when I found my dad. He helped me prepare the dinner we shared, was with me when I was told he was dead, and when I went to identify the body. The friendship turned into a loving relationship, and approximately a year later we married. Our first child, Jasmine, was born in 1985. Our son, Malcolm, was born in 1987. We divorced in 1999.

The transition from marriage to divorce was the most difficult because of the impact on my children. I will never forget the look in Malcolm's eyes at the time we told them. Jasmine had a nonchalant attitude. It was her defense mechanism. How well do preteens and teens comprehend the concept of their parents growing apart? We had done well by them and for them to this point. However, we did not know how to be married to the people we both had become and were becoming. Neither one of us witnessed healthy marriages in our households as children. I believe that my prior trauma was a consideration in the marriage ending, but not in the ways that some would think. I have come to realize that sometimes when people have feelings of invisibility, abandonment, and betrayal when they are young, they have little tolerance for it as an adult in any form. We sought counseling, utilizing three different counselors (two as a couple, and one as a family). It wasn't enough. That was a painful reality for all of us. The two things Jasmine and Malcolm needed to know was that we both loved them and that the divorce wasn't their fault. In recent years, I have held conversations with both of my children and they each have said how thankful they were for how their dad and I shaped their lives. Granville and I have remained cordial. As adults, our children know that things do not always work out the way we think they will.

Permanent Housing

I had two conversations with the Salvation Army's case managers while I was a resident. One, was a member of the church I attended. We had first connected in Sunday School before my days at the shelter. Seeing her coming out of her office at the Salvation Army while I was in a most vulnerable state was a trigger for me. I would discover that reconciling the feelings and thoughts about my homelessness and what others would think, particularly people who knew me through other settings would be crucial to my purpose. There was no room for ego. Nor would there be any room for shame, fear, or guilt. I could not let what other people might think about me, or the letters in front or behind my name, silence me regarding my experience, or deter me from the path I was being drawn to.

Coming to this realization helped me frame the conversations with Jasmine and Malcolm when the decision was made to share my story, and to do homeless advocacy work. I knew that the power of my story would be in its authenticity, and my willingness to be made vulnerable. My vulnerability involved opening up about my homelessness in ways that forced me to fully understand the situation beyond self, and to challenge the status quo. I not only needed to share my personal experience of homelessness, but I needed to be active in promoting transformative change to end homelessness. The approach had to take us beyond charity. As an advocate for people experiencing homelessness, being formerly homeless had to become a salient aspect of my identity, an important aspect of who I am. This would not be to gain pity, or for people to feel sorry for me, but rather to dismantle stereotypes about who is homeless.

The Salvation Army helped with my security deposit. I needed to secure the first month's rent for an apartment. My anticipated pension would provide that, and the additional income needed to pay a monthly rent. Looking for an apartment was a reminder of another reality. Some landlords did not want to rent to people who did not have earned income from a job. This translated to people with pensions, disability checks, housing vouchers, or some other form of income being susceptible to housing discrimination. I would learn that people were denied housing due to their source of income. Another consideration was also a history of evictions, negative credit check reports, and types of previous addresses. Having a homeless shelter as your last residence could work against you. I was the poster child for all the aforementioned. Although my eviction had left a judgment against me and I was moving out of a shelter, during March 2012, I moved into an apartment in Wilmington, Delaware. I now know I was one of the lucky ones.

The apartment was in a two-story house with one unit on the first floor, and two units on the second floor. I lived in one of the units on the second floor. My apartment kitchen and living area windows faced downtown Wilmington. I was walking distance to Market Street, the main shopping and banking area, and Rodney Square, a park and central public transportation hub, and space where people identified as homeless would spend time. Rodney Square was known for its concerts, festivals, and outdoor markets. I was also within walking distance of Trolley Square, a neighborhood known for its nightlife, and a known hang out for young people. Coming out of the shelter, I now lived on a quiet street of private homes and apartment buildings between those two realities.

I had no furniture. I had sold or given it all away during the eviction process. I spent that first afternoon unpacking the boxes from my car. After two months, I could finally drive around Delaware and Philadelphia without hauling possessions. I now had space, if needed, for others to ride with me. My friend Renee drove from Middletown with her air mattress, letting me know that I had use of it as long as needed. She was the first person to enter my "home" after leaving the shelter. The apartment was cozy with much light. Perfect for the plants I expected to retrieve from Carolyn in a few days. The times I visited with her, I could see they were growing beautifully in her care. Karen, her dad, and one of her daughters dropped the cats off. She and her daughter carried them up the stairs, and our conversation was about how well they had behaved themselves, and how much they were going to be missed. Once out of their carriers, they both looked at me, and began to explore the apartment. They were a little distant for a day or two. They got over it.

The apartment's best feature for me was its huge bathroom with its claw foot bathtub. I remember yearning for the serenity of taking an aromatic soak, something that I had not done in a while. Certainly, bath bubbles, candles, and a glass of wine were on the agenda in the near future. The first night in the apartment, I was so grateful to be in my own place. No roommates. No chores or curfews. No concerns about missing property. With my back against the bedroom wall looking at the darkness of the night sky through the window on the opposite wall, I sat on the floor quietly thinking about the journey. Then I cried.

Over the next few weeks, I paid my previous landlord the $623.00 owed in back rent, plus court fees. I made a donation to my church in the amount they had given me to help with my rent as a special offering, with the request that the monies would be utilized to continue to help others who needed financial assistance with housing. A financial advisor from my banking institution called me to discuss my portfolio. What a difference a month made. The increased funds in my account put me on their radar. The pension allowed me to pay my rent on time and in full for the remainder of 2012. I would continue to look for full-time work, teach my online university courses, and begin to think about how to give voice to my experience with homelessness in Delaware.

Next Steps

Not too long after moving into the apartment I received a call from Kim. It was the first time connecting with her since leaving the shelter. She shared that she had been surviving on the streets, after being forced to leave the Salvation Army shelter following an incident with shelter staff. The police were called to take her to a mental health facility, but she refused to go, and my understanding was that they could not make her go. She was upset because the public exchange with the shelter staff exposed her issue with mental illness and she felt disrespected, shamed, humiliated, and hurt. I sensed she also felt betrayed.

Instead of going to the mental health facility, Kim found her way to Rodney Square where she slept on a bench. It rained heavily that night. She shared the indignity of being propositioned by men while fighting the elements, and the feeling of being disposable. Her story further confirmed for me that there was something fundamentally wrong with the emergency housing system in Delaware, and with a society that demonized those living with mental health issues, and those who were identified as homeless. I believed I related to her not only because of the shared experience of shelter homelessness, but because of having a dad who lived with mental illness. I was reminded of the social stigma, prejudice, fear, and family silence I had been conditioned to internalize about him. I have come to understand silence to be not only not speaking up or speaking about something, but also to be a willful ignoring of individuals, actions, and situations. I understand the most powerful aspect about silence to be how it blurred or made invisible truth.

As I listened to her story, I thought I understood her feeling of powerlessness, as I imagined my dad may have felt it. I knew the feeling of stigma and fear as the child of a parent who lived with mental illness, and who was periodically hospitalized. I remember the sense of relief when I eventually learned that I had a 13% chance of being diagnosed paranoid schizophrenic. That is when I chose to focus on the 87% of not having the diagnosis. Before then, I would wonder if what happened to my dad would happen to me. I also wondered if people thought I was like my dad. I became a psychologist to learn more about my dad, and to help people like him. I realized shortly after my first social psychology class, that I did not want to be a clinician, but rather someone who helped answer questions and solve problems related to diverse people and broader societal issues. Now, I had an experiential connection to people identified as homeless, and a greater awareness of yet another stigmatized identity, people without housing security.

We talked about what she could do, and the decision was made to write a letter of complaint to the national and regional leadership of the Salvation Army about how she had been treated. I offered her my place to come to take a shower if she needed. I do not remember her showing up, but we did have subsequent phone conversations to develop her letter, and within a few days, the letter was sent. I purposely did not write the letter for her. It was important that Kim knew what she was empowered to do for herself. We lost contact over the years. I hope she is well. This situation was the tipping point for my advocacy addressing the disempowerment, hopelessness, silencing, indignities, and inhumanity visited upon people experiencing homelessness. It was time for something different in Delaware.

I started the journey to identify advocacy groups that specifically protected the rights of people experiencing homelessness in Delaware. There were none. I did a computer search for a homeless bill of rights in Delaware. There was no information. However, I did discover that the idea was not a new one, and that a homeless bill of rights had been passed in Rhode Island. Also, other cities and states were working on similar legislation. It was a pleasant surprise to discover that others were focused on the human rights of people identified as homeless.

My research helped me identify an organization working with homelessness in Delaware, called the Homeless Planning Council. I sent an email asking, "Is there a homeless bill of rights for the state of Delaware?" The response was no. However, I was invited to come in to have a conversation with the agency's executive director. A few days later, I was sharing my story of homelessness, and how the experience revealed the need for more to be done to protect the rights of people without housing. I left that meeting with the promise that a larger meeting with community stakeholders would convene where we could explore it further. That second and larger meeting did take place. At that second meeting, I would be reunited with Rhonda Celester, a former resident from the Salvation Army shelter who I had befriended, and would be introduced to Charles Johnson, founder of H.A.R.P. (Homeless People Are Real People Too), who was also formerly homeless. It would be at this meeting that the first community group conversation would be held exploring a homeless bill of rights for Delaware.

The next few weeks would see the development of the Policy Committee on Ending Homelessness in Delaware (A Working Group of the Homeless Planning Council of Delaware), to develop a white paper exploring the issues of homeless discrimination, criminalization, and to offer policy suggestions. I was be one of its eight committee members, and a contributor to the paper.

I would become a community supporter of H.A.R.P., working with the group to bring deeper awareness about homelessness in Delaware. I participated in the group's community forum, which brought together the city of Wilmington's mayoral candidates to discuss their plans for addressing homelessness and provided an opportunity for community members to express needs, concerns, and expectations. The meeting was held in a space known as the Creative Vision Factory (CVF), an art studio for people living with behavioral health disorders, and in recovery from substance abuse. H.A.R.P. held its meetings there as well, and some members participated in the activities at CVF. I never worked with a group like H.A.R.P. I was an outsider. I was currently housed, some of H.A.R.P. members were not. Most of H.A.R.P. members were in recovery, I was not. However, we connected around advocacy for people who were experiencing homelessness. All of us had homelessness as a shared experience.

I had a front row seat as the five candidates offered a variety of approaches to addressing homelessness in Wilmington. They each agreed that there was a problem. As usual, fingers were pointed to others that should or could be doing more to address the issue. I quickly realized that I was connecting with different stakeholders around the issue of homelessness from community advocates with lived experience to organizations and agencies that were receiving state and federal funds to support shelters, transitional housing, and programs geared toward the homeless. I felt like I was entering a space that would provide information to help my cause. I was learning.

Because of the energy around the quest for Delaware's homeless bill of rights, I was contacted by Delaware's NPR News for a second interview. A reporter was sent to my apartment, and I was interviewed for a story on my experience with homelessness and growing advocacy work. I was asked to describe the shelter, and I shared my feelings of uncertainty and anxiety living with strangers for thirty days. I spoke about the need for a homeless bill of rights to stop discrimination against people identified as homeless. I shared that I wanted the "Delaware bill to be based on empowering homeless people to advocate for themselves." The title of the news story was "Turning homelessness into a call for action" and it would be the first time that my story of homelessness and call for a homeless bill of rights for the State of Delaware would be shared through the media. The article, written by Jon Hurdle was published September, 2012. Reviewing the article years later, I fully recognized the trauma I had experienced.

That December, I was asked to speak at H.A.R.P.'s first annual heroes and heroines' awards program. I submitted Karen Summa's name to be considered for one of the awards for her thoughtful gesture in caring for my cats while I was sheltered. I shared our story before she was presented her award. The new year presented an opportunity to be a speaker on the Service Providers Panel on Homelessness and Peer Support at the Delaware Case Management Training Program: Best Practices in Homeless Services meeting sponsored by the Homeless Planning Council of Delaware. After sharing my story and speaking about a homeless bill of rights, a young, male, African American social worker raised his hand and said, "It's my hope that you did not have negative encounters. If so, I want to apologize." I felt his sincerity, and responded, "No, but too many others have." His comment led to another social worker, an African American female, standing up, and through tears she said, "Thank you for sharing because right now I'm facing eviction. I'm seeing people every day, and I'm facing the same situation. I'm too embarrassed to let people, especially those I work with, know what I'm going through." The room was silent. I left that panel discussion knowing that there was much to be done in addressing systemic and structural barriers to the empowerment of people experiencing homelessness, and at risk of homelessness.

DeBorah Gilbert White, PhD.

Shortly after that gathering the policy committee's white paper "Ending Discrimination for Delaware's Homeless-Protecting the Rights of Our Most Vulnerable Citizens" was released. I would find myself accompanying members of H.A.R.P to participate in a conversation with the director and deputy director of Delaware's Department of Health and Social Services. It would be here that I would assist H.A.R.P. in introducing cultural proficiency as a tool to address issues community members had shared about engaging social services in Delaware, and to support service providers in their work.

It was only a year earlier that I was a resident in a shelter. Now, that experience provided me with a voice. That voice would be utilized to clearly and boldly proclaim that people experiencing homelessness mattered. Working with H.A.R.P. in community, we sponsored a press conference in Wilmington, Delaware in response to the city's decision to stop people experiencing homelessness from selling the *Our Independence Newspaper* on the streets. The next day the local newspaper story headline read "Paper Hawkers Cling To Hope." Yes, there were some problems due mainly to a lack of structure connected to where papers were being sold, and complaints from downtown business owners about vendor conduct. Although the problems were valid, I now realize ending the street sales of the paper was yet another way, intentional or not, to make invisible the unhoused and their needs.

Street vending of newspapers by people experiencing homelessness nationally and globally was a source of revenue, and a proven vehicle for the self-empowerment of many to meet economic needs. The decision prompted me to write two letters to the mayor, one before the press conference and one after. Working with H.A.R.P. members, I compiled and wrote the "Newspaper Street Vendors Training Manual" to assist with rectifying the concerns raised. I did receive a response from the Mayor's office of Economic

Development. The city was standing firm on its decision. It became clearer that the empowerment of people identified as homeless in Wilmington was going to be an uphill battle. Writing the letter to support people selling the newspaper was my first engagement with city leadership, but it would not be my last.

During this time, I was also exploring what was happening on the national level connected to homelessness. This is when I became familiar with the National Coalition for the Homeless (NCH), the National Law Center on Homelessness and Poverty (NLCHP), both in Washington, D.C., and would learn more about the efforts of others around the country related to homeless advocacy. In later years, NLCHP would change its name to the National Homelessness Law Center. It would also be the time that I would become aware of work toward a national homeless bill of rights. I requested materials from NCH and NLCHP and eventually would reach out to the National Coalition for the Homeless on behalf of Homeless Are Real People Too (H.A.R.P.) to connect with their speakers' bureau. I had proposed to H.A. R. P. that we develop local speakers to support the homeless advocacy work we were doing in Delaware, and NCH could assist us.

Reflections

Shortly after coming out of homelessness, I was asked, "Would you have the same energy for the issue if you had not been homeless?" The question caused me at the time to reflect on the path I had taken, to where I then found myself as a community advocate on the issue. The seed for advocacy work connected to people experiencing homelessness was planted years before I experienced it. My professional training and work were associated with diversity and inclusion, and the exploration of social power and privilege, the making of in-groups and out-groups, the role of perceptions, stereotypes, and stigma in human relationships. Each of the aforementioned connected to the issue of homelessness, and to people identified as homeless. I could answer the question honestly yes, understanding that inequity and injustice needed to be addressed in whatever form it presented itself.

As a child and teenager, I held a strong sense about the treatment of people because of who they were. I believe that sensitivity came about because of the way I saw the adults around me handle the mental health issues of my father. The experience with my dad's mental illness shaped me as a person in two fundamental ways. First, it allowed me to know the effects of social stigma on individuals living with a mental illness, and the people connected to them. Second, it brought to the forefront how we as individuals and families can treat those we perceive as different. Both provided insights that wired me emotionally and psychologically to look at and work with diversity and inclusion issues in a nonjudgmental way, which allowed for meaningful engagement with diverse individuals and groups. Religious beliefs, sexual orientation, class considerations, among other things, were simply not a barrier for me.

In subsequent years, I would begin to understand this concept as it related to race and racism in the United States and globally. The death of Dr. Martin Luther King, Jr. left me feeling bewildered. As an eleven-year-old child, I remember asking my grandmother, "Why would someone want to kill somebody that just wanted to help people?" It would be many years later, as a young adult and mother, that I would be introduced in a transformative way to the concepts of social justice and social change. It would be an awakening that allowed the intertwining of my faith and need for active participation in making the world a better place.

I was nearing the end of maternity leave for my second child and was not looking forward to returning to a position as a telephone operator at a major Wall Street brokerage firm. I'm amazed even now, at how fluidly each of the firm's five partner's names rolled off my tongue each time I answered the phone. The work had become mundane, I was not being challenged intellectually, and motherhood was pushing me to think more about the future. I was sensing that I could do more and was also contemplating returning to school to complete my undergraduate degree. The decision was made not to return to the brokerage firm, but to work for a temp agency to continue to bring income into the household. A girlfriend who worked at a temporary agency called one day with a job. She indicated that it was a receptionist position, located on Madison Avenue in New York City; however, it was working for a church. She wanted to know if I would be interested. I responded, "I don't know, girl. Let me think about that one."

We both laughed at the job being at a church. Currently, neither one of us attended church regularly, if at all. She was an aspiring singer, spending her Sunday's sleeping after club dates on Saturday nights. I had long ago given up on organized religion, and on obligatory thinking about needing to be in a particular space or place on Sunday mornings. I did not find the church relevant for me or the issues of the day, particularly its messages of fear and "fire and brimstone" that had been drilled into me as a child. I was made to fear God to the point that I could not love God. When I added a sense of betrayal by God, I was done. Years later, I would mourn the lack of understanding about being in relationship with God due to bad theology, and the disillusionment resulting from experiences with people connected to the church that today would lead me to say "Me Too." In so many ways, the church represented hurt. However, with all that emotional, psychological, and spiritual baggage I told her yes. At that time, I did not know how that "yes" would change my life forever. I continue to be thankful for the presence of mind on that day to try something new and to stretch my boundaries. I now know it was God.

My friend was partially right. The position was not in a church building as I envisioned, but in an office building where the national headquarters or offices of a denomination known as the United Church of Christ (UCC) was located. Not only was the position at the church's denominational offices, but it was also located in its social justice ministries. The temporary assignment was in its civil rights arm, an office called the Commission for Racial Justice (CRJ). After several weeks answering phones, greeting visitors, making copies, I was immersed into the work of CRJ. Although the denomination was predominately White, the Commission for Racial Justice had predominantly Black staff and leadership. CRJ also had two regional offices, one in Whitakers, NC, and the other in Washington, D.C. It was my first experience working with people that looked like me who held and owned their power, who loved and fought for Blacks, and other people of color within and outside a faith community.

DeBorah Gilbert White, PhD.

Each day presented new information and understanding of the role a person's faith could have in making the world a better place. This was a revelation for me. I was someone who had been taught to feel "powerless" and that my only option was to pray about troubling, negative, or bad situations. I had been nurtured with "pie in the sky" theology. However, something within me told me there was more that could be done, here on earth, and that it could be done now. As I reflect, I know that God (not the one that I was so afraid of) was always with me. It was a God of protection of my ability to have hope, no matter what life was throwing my way. It was the same God at age seven, age eleven, age fifty-five, and every age in between, that allowed me to hold on for the better that was yet to come. I now recognize that over the years, living with the mindset of a survivor and not a victim was my saving grace.

The Commission for Racial Justice was a special place. The office walls featured large portrait size black and white photos of the civil rights causes the church, through the work CRJ, had been a part of. The pictures spoke a thousand words in depicting marches for voting rights, activists protesting against toxic wastes dumping in poor and Black communities, leadership, staff and community members at a newly dedicated women's shelter, and one of Dr. Charles Cobb, CRJ's emeritus executive director, and one of the denomination's trailblazing clergy and racial justice activists sitting at his desk. It was here that I learned that the United Church of Christ had provided money to provide bail for Angela Davis, a member of the Black Panther Party. It was here that I learned about the Wilmington 10, met and worked alongside Dr. Benjamin F. Chavis, Jr., a member of the Wilmington 10, who was now a UCC minister and the executive director of the Commission for Racial Justice. It would be here that I formed a friendship with Judy Richardson, a former member of the Student Nonviolent Coordinating Committee (SNCC) who as a college student participated in voter registration and student sit-ins across the country. Judy would later become a producer for the documentary *Eyes On The Prize*. It would be here that I met and learned from community activists like Dollie Burwell, the mother of the environmental justice movement. It was here where I would meet a young woman working with the children of families identified as homeless living in New York City's welfare hotels, who would be known years later as raptivist and author Sister Souljah. At that time, homelessness and its emerging issues were not on my radar. My picture of homelessness were the men I would see sitting, standing, and laying on the streets, generally when I was coming out of the subway on my way to work. It was 1988, and I could not know how much promoting housing as a human right and addressing homelessness would be an integral part of my life's work in the years to come.

At the Commission for Racial Justice I would learn to connect local, national, and international struggles for social justice. I would come to know that God's work was as much about what justice could be done on earth, as it was about obtaining eternal life. I came to recognize how deeply I felt about developing awareness, providing education, and eliminating the oppression of individuals and members of groups simply because of their identity. It would be here that I would begin to grow.

Eventually I was offered a permanent position at the Commission for Racial Justice to assist Judy Richardson, its communication director, and to do other duties as assigned. I said yes, again, and was incorporated fully into social justice work, and making a difference in the world. To date, I have never experienced a workplace like CRJ. It was diverse and inclusive, affirming, and empowering. I grew to love the work and people to the point that Friday came too soon, and Monday could not come soon enough. One day, while sitting at my desk, I laughed out loud, looked toward the ceiling, and thought, "God you got me!" I realized that I was now spending five days at the "church" when for so long, I wouldn't spend one.

Besides doing research for CRJ's weekly newsletter and radio segment *Civil Rights Journal* I managed the newsletter mailing list, was the liaison between the office and Black press across the country, scheduled the weekly studio tapings of the "Journal" and coordinated the weekly mailing. One of the other duties as assigned was responding to requests for the newly published report *Toxic Wastes and Race In The United States*. This 1987 landmark report identified how race was a factor in how companies were dumping cancer causing toxic wastes in poor, and predominantly people of color communities. At the time I did not fully understand the significance of the report, or how, many years later I would be sharing that significance with members of the sociology classes I facilitated on cultural diversity for the University of Phoenix. Again, I would find myself engaging others in exploring social justice and equity issues connected to group identity. A lens that would be foundational to my research and advocacy work in the years to come.

Community Activism and Advocacy

The United Church of Christ made the decision to move its national offices to Cleveland, Ohio. I was offered an opportunity to relocate with them. The offer to move came with an incentive package that allowed our young family to own a home. Cleveland would be the place where my political awareness and advocacy would be heightened through community involvement. It began with doing voter registration in a section of the city known as Hough. The first political campaign I would be part of would be for the re-election of Hough's beloved Councilwoman, Fannie Lewis. Hough was a predominantly African American community that was historically known for its riots in 1966. Councilwoman Lewis worked to address the generational impact of the riots, and to support political and economic growth in Hough. As a former welfare recipient, she fought tirelessly for those identified as low-income and poor.

I and others met at her house often to learn about politics and community empowerment. I was in awe of the councilwoman. There was nothing pretentious about her. When I met her in the late 1990's, she was a grayed-haired senior, often wearing her wide skirts, with a tee-shirt and sneakers as she connected with her constituents in the community. Councilwoman Lewis was the first community person I knew personally holding a political position. She had no problem asking the hard questions. Unapologetically, she was African American, tough, and genuinely committed to her work and to her community. She said, "We have a responsibility to do what we can for each other," and she lived by that.

While working in community with Councilwoman Lewis, and as an undergraduate and graduate student at Cleveland State University (CSU), I was involved in the formation of a student activist group. We called ourselves Positive Action Coalition (PAC) and were advised by CSU political science professor Muhammad Ahmad (aka Maxwell Stanford, Jr.). A former Black Panther and leader of RAM (Revolutionary Action Movement), his guidance provided insight into past community justice struggles, and the importance of building coalitions to address societal injustice. He was also a resident of Hough. We became volunteers for Councilwoman Lewis. Another member of that group was Nina Turner. She would rise to serve as a Senator from Ohio, become a key supporter working with the Bernie Sanders' presidential campaigns, and a political commentator. We spent much time knocking on doors, meeting people in the Hough community of Cleveland, and registering people to vote. This community work and connecting with grassroots organizations further confirmed for me the power of the vote, and the importance of the voices of people in the community.

My work with the United Church of Christ engaged me in the church's ministry connected to reparations for the enslavement of Africans in the United States. At that time, I held the position of Minister for Anti-Racism and Conflict Resolution. In 2001, the UCC passed the resolution "A Call for a Study on Reparations for Slavery", and in 2002, the Justice and Witness Ministries Reparations Working Group convened. Reverend Adora Iris Lee and I were assigned as staff to this group led by Dr. Iva Carruthers, subject matter expert and author of *The Church and Reparations*. The work would propel me to connecting with and building relationship with members of Cleveland's city government, the

Beyond Charity

Greater Cleveland Mobilization Coalition Inter-faith Committee, organizations working for reparations across the country, particularly N'COBRA (The National Coalition of Blacks for Reparations in America), and the office of Congressman John Conyers in Washington D.C. (sponsor of the legislation). We were working to expand awareness, education, and support for H.R.40, known as *The Commission to Study Reparations Proposal for African Americans Act*. This would be my first work with legislation.

Adora and I served as editors for the UCC's Reparations Working Group resource *Reparations: A Process for Repairing The Breach* which was presented to the denomination the summer of 2003. That fall, Dr. Iva Carruthers and I represented the United Church of Christ at the Congressional Black Caucus' Legislative Conference "Reparations Forum 2003: Honoring The Debt." As I reflect on these experiences, I come to realize that I have crossed paths with people, particularly women, who were deeply committed to the empowerment of others. I would realize years later how the lessons learned would be fundamental to shaping my efforts to address society's inequities connected to homelessness, and the knowledge that I was empowered to bring about change. It is clear, the issues I care about are those that speak to society's marginalized individuals and groups and call for promoting social justice and social change.

A few years ago, I became familiar with the definition of advocacy as changing "what is into what should be." The boldness of this definition continues to support the feeling of urgency and empowerment experienced in the work for social change. I know what the cost and the resulting collateral damage of not having an advocate, or not being able to advocate for self can be. In some sense, I think that coming through some of my life's most difficult experiences taught me the importance of being an advocate for self, in preparation to advocate for others.

The Politics of Homelessness

I often reflect on how the issues that are important to or valued in society have legislation to support and protect them. When social issues arise as a reflection of society's diversity or lack of social inclusion, and when historically marginalized individuals and members of groups expect the same rights and privileges as others, those issues evolve and so does our politics. We see this in the fight for civil rights, women's rights, and marriage equality. Most recently, we see it in the response to police brutality and the Black Lives Matter call to dismantle systemic racism. I know that call involves our housing and homeless provider systems as well.

The first engagement I had with Delaware legislators was to share my story and to bring more focus to homeless prevention. Where were the preventive services for people like me, those who could not check any of the boxes to receive social services? I wanted to know, did I and others like me matter? Not having adequate monies and services geared toward prevention with an increasing eviction and homelessness rate is a political move. The lingering question would be why? I now understand that part of the answer lies in what people holding political power have the political will to address.

I believed I was being called to be part of the change for how people identified as homeless were perceived, treated, and empowered. The work toward a homeless bill of rights for Delaware was indeed a process that would introduce me to a world that I did not know. A large portion of the battle was to counter the myths and stereotypes about homelessness, and to get people in key power positions to view people experiencing homelessness as constituents, with the same rights and protections as all others in a society that did not have a stigmatized homeless identity. This involved engaging service providers, law enforcement, landlords, and legislators in ways that expanded the narrative and understanding about the issue, and about the people. Greater emphasis on the people.

On June 11, 2014, State Representative Stephanie Bolden introduced HB378, An Act To Amend Title 6 Of The Delaware Code Relating To Homeless Persons to the Housing & Community Affairs Committee during the 147th General Assembly of the House of Representatives, State of Delaware. Co-sponsors of the bill were Senators Robert Marshall, Bryan Townsend, and Margaret Rose Henry, and Representatives Helene Keeley, and Charles Potter, Jr. This would be the first legislative effort community advocates viewed as an outgrowth of the stakeholders meeting held approximately two years prior, exploring a Homeless Bill of Rights for Delaware. Unfortunately, people from the community who were experiencing homelessness, formerly homeless, or at risk of homelessness were not there. The community people who worked on developing the Homeless Planning Council's Working Group white paper, and community people connected to homeless advocacy were not in the room. The meeting minutes indicate that the conversation would have been enriched and more informative if the folks who initially asked for such legislation were present in the room. It was another missed opportunity for legislators and community members to work together on such an important issue. Intentional or not, the politics of homelessness decided which voices were heard, which people were visible, and which were not.

Another challenge was to change the mindset of many people experiencing homelessness, service providers, and others doing homeless outreach. The primary narrative concerning people experiencing homelessness was that not having housing was an indication of a lack of personal fortitude or some character flaw. The narrative promoted the image of people sleeping and surviving on the streets, men and women pushing shopping carts, living in cardboard boxes, in the woods, or under bridges. Yes, those images are real in sharing the reality of some of society's most vulnerable human beings without housing. However, those images provide a view of the tip of the iceberg when it comes to homelessness. They are the images that are the most visible, haunting, and telling of the failure to eradicate the lack of housing in one of the most developed countries in the world.

It is important to know that most people identified as homeless, we never see. People like me who doubled-up with a family member, those living in shelters, or vehicles, transitional housing, and couch surfers, are not easily seen. Many of the people experiencing homelessness are women and children, youth, particularly youth identifying as LGBT (lesbian, gay, bisexual, transgender), and college students. Many people experiencing homelessness work. Expanding the narrative about homelessness and who is homeless continues to be key to addressing the issue. How we define and view the issue and the people impacted shapes how we respond.

Fundamentally, there continues to be a need to move the narrative away from the belief purported consciously and unconsciously that the experience of homelessness is the result of sin, placing causation on the actions and behaviors of individuals, and the view of poverty as a generational curse, without considering other factors such as pathology, or social issues beyond the people impacted. There is no consideration of society's generational oppression or lack of access and opportunities for many people. As hard as I try, I cannot identify the sin I committed that led to my job loss, protracted limited income, and eventual homelessness. Promoting the bootstrap mentality for people without boots or straps, and tying outreach to vulnerable people laden with evangelism is predatory when people's stomachs are empty, and they are experiencing homelessness because of the lack of a living wage, and availability of low-income, descent, safe, and secure housing. The politics of homelessness encourages us to turn our attention away from societal and personal barriers impacting access and opportunities, and from calling policymakers on every level into accountability. In my eyes, hunger and homelessness are more moral and social problems, than spiritual ones. Basically, it is about having and showing humanity, and meeting the needs of fellow human beings, without trampling on their humanity, dignity, and rights.

The politics of homelessness does not uncover the embedded societal prejudices, biases, perceptions about homelessness, and what people experiencing homelessness internalized based on it. Many are accepting of systemic policies, practices, and procedures that diminish their dignity and humanity. The internalization leads some to believe they deserve being without housing or to feeling powerless to address what they are experiencing as mistreatment, disrespect, and unfair or over-reaching policies and practices from those providing the basic needs of shelter, food, and clothing. This leads us to reflect on the ways people identified as poor, and people experiencing homelessness, are demonized and criminalized. When society declares sitting, eating, standing, and other human functions in public crimes, then what are people to do when they have no other place to go or to be?

After social service agencies, churches and other faith-based groups and organizations are the next stop for people seeking help with food and housing. It is problematic when people in need encounter people in these spaces who want to help, but who are not adequately equipped to do so. It really does take more than having a good heart and being a good person to engage people at a most vulnerable time in their lives in ways that do not perpetuate additional harm. People engaging in outreach or social services need to do their own work identifying how they feel, or what they believe about poverty, and about people experiencing homelessness. We do more harm with our good intentions, when we have not unpacked our own stereotypes, biases, prejudices, and judgement.

There is no shortage of disturbing stories connected to the treatment of people identified as homeless. There are intentional and unintentional, conscious, and subconscious ways we dehumanize others. Stories have been shared with me on the journey to protect the dignity and humanity of people identified as homeless. Some have felt bullied into giving up their food stamps to providers, with no say in the food choices for them to eat. Their complaints or concerns about high sodium, lack of green vegetables, and food quality were often met with retaliation. Some have shared stories of unsanitary and unclean living conditions. Places and spaces identified to house individuals and families were reported to have old tattered and torn furniture, dirty and stained carpets, and needing a fresh coat of paint. I had my own to reflect on as a shelter resident. There are continual complaints about service providers being hostile and rude in their encounters with people seeking and receiving services. A volunteer at one of the area's largest shelters spoke to the insulting and dehumanizing way its residents were spoken to. She was appalled.

One woman shared with me being intimidated by shelter staff. She witnessed baby diapers and other items going out the door. She was told to "Keep her mouth shut and mind her own business" when she spoke up about donations to the shelter being taken by shelter staff rather than being provided to shelter residents to management. She also had complained about poor case management. The conversation ended with her being told that she was "Skating on thin ice" which put her in a state of uncertainty about maintaining shelter, and not feeling safe. She felt that the unwritten rules were: "Mind your business, don't speak on anything you see, turn your head, and lie about resources they provided." There was no one or no place to share such concerns that she trusted.

I received a handwritten two-page letter from a person working at a shelter for women and children (not the same one I lived in for thirty days). She was disturbed by the lack of professionalism exhibited by her fellow staff members, inadequate staff coverage, and other safety concerns at the facility for workers and residents. When a co-worker shared with her that "The people that come here do not want change" she recognized that the work environment was not the proper one for her. In her letter she stated, "My vision for serving people is far above what I witnessed there. Through that experience I have learned how not to treat human beings."

A woman living in a shelter prior to having surgery was told a few days after returning from the hospital that she would no longer have a bed. She spoke to the anxiety and emotional toll the situation presented for her. She was in the process of healing, with stitches and on meds, and trying to focus on getting well. With limited options for housing, she was able to identify a friend who took her in while she got better. She developed a stuttering problem, which she attributed to the multiple stressful experiences she encountered while experiencing homelessness. I became aware of two cases connected to men experiencing homelessness, who were diagnosed with cancer. In both cases the hospitals could not release them to the streets. One, whose cancer was in an advanced stage, was given one of the 12 beds in a private hospice unit at Christiana Care Hospital in Newark, DE, where a few weeks later he died. The other, who needed to receive outpatient cancer treatments, was provided a voucher to an area motel. Not the most ideal situation, but the best that could be offered under the circumstances. It saddened me to know that there was no place for people identified as homeless to go within the shelter system for respite care.

People identified as poor and people experiencing homelessness do not need for others to feel "sorry" for them, or to "save" them. Instead, people identified as poor and people experiencing homelessness need people to empathize with them, and more importantly to work for, or alongside them to address societal injustices that impact the lack of low-income housing, a living or housing wage to be able to pay rent, and to stop the demonizing and criminalization of poverty and homelessness. People who are housed live with the same issues that people experiencing homelessness do. Yet, for the most part, they are not demonized or criminalized. We have made the stereotypes of homelessness, reflected in the images of people living on the streets, perceived as drug and alcohol abusers, and people living with mental illness as the majority of people who are without housing. They are not. We must expand the narrative about homelessness and who is homeless to address homelessness and its emerging issues in a holistic way. How do we tell the full story?

The politics of homelessness supports a society that works for people who have housing. It should. Understanding housing as a human right and not a privilege or commodity; we all should have a place to live, and to have our dignity and humanity protected when we don't. The politics of homelessness stokes the disdain, judgement, lack of empathy, and criminalization many people with housing hold for people experiencing homelessness, especially those surviving on the streets. The dominant privileged mindset in politics regarding homelessness often undergirds values, perceptions, attitudes, and beliefs of some (the housed), and diminishes the dignity and humanity of others (the unhoused). Such attitudes and mindset challenge the efforts of homeless advocates.

In the politics of homelessness privilege is exercised in various ways. Privilege allows supportive homeless legislation to die in committee, blocks the establishment of a tiny house village, bans people asking for help from their neighborhood or city, jails and fines people experiencing homelessness who we know can't make bail, and allows landlords to evict people without representation, too often a retaliatory action that results in homelessness. It is a mindset that people experiencing homelessness, housing instability, and poverty cannot afford.

The Homeless Industrial Complex

Like all other social justice issues, there are those who benefit from the inequities connected to housing or the lack of housing in a society directly or indirectly. During a conversation on the matter with Michael Stoops, who at the time was acting executive director of the National Coalition for the Homeless, and founder of its Faces of Homeless Speakers Bureau, he asked, "How many sandwiches would we need to continue to make?" It is a question that I continue to reflect on today, as efforts to address homelessness feels like pouring water into a bucket riddled with holes. There seems to be more effort to manage homelessness rather than end it, and not enough effort to prevent it.

The sentiment was that as advocates for people living in poverty, facing hunger, and experiencing homelessness, we needed to find ways to address hunger and homelessness that ultimately brings an end to how we have come to know it. I shared with Michael that I thought we needed a change in mindset in Delaware. We needed more of a mindset where people were more focused on working themselves out of a job, rather than patting themselves on the back for how long they have been doing charity work and feeling comfortable positioning themselves to continue band aid solutions, rather than envisioning an end to this form of human suffering.

There was still much to be done to live in a society and world that worked for everyone. On the surface it seemed unconscionable to think that people did not have housing, lived in shelters, slept on the streets, or other uninhabitable spaces, and could not afford to pay rent in what was deemed the most advanced and powerful country in the world. How could that be? What kept that situation in place? What did that say about the systems set up to address the issue?

I have come to understand that there is money in poverty, and that the homeless industrial complex is real. I have come to understand it in two forms, both predatory, and both supportive of the status quo. It would not be until I attended the National Law Center on Homelessness and Poverty "Housing Is A Human Right" Conference in 2018, that I would first hear the term "Homeless Industrial Complex" and would begin to fully understand how it worked. The term helped me to make sense of why we as communities, cities, states, and a country cannot or will not end homelessness.

One of the ways it operates is by drawing people who are experiencing homelessness and housing insecurity, the marginalized, into a web that becomes difficult to escape, and where a sub-economy flourishes based on that marginalization. This is evident in businesses like payday and title loans, rent to own, storage companies, check cashing and financial services options for those who cannot qualify for traditional banking institutions. Getting what you need comes at a higher cost. Another way it works is through a combination of city governments, businesses, developers, and philanthropists partnering with nonprofits in ways that maintain the status quo.

A conversation with Evelyn, a woman who left a career in the nonprofit sector, was evidence of the toll the homeless industrial complex has on people doing the work, who become uncomfortable with what they see, and want to change the status quo. She left a well-paying position when she experienced what she says was "poverty more valued than people," which she determined as what made it difficult to solve the homeless problem. Evelyn's career spanned the community economic development spectrum, including work in transitional housing, financial education, and coaching. Like me, she experienced the system to be paternalistic and existing on the dehumanization of the poor. She described it as being on a "hamster wheel" and was frustrated with the racial disparity among the decision making and leadership positions of most organizations working with homelessness. Evelyn called the homeless industrial complex a "Jobs program for White people." Managing the problem, rather than ending the problem continues to provide income and work for many people, most of them White. Again, where was the incentive to change that?

From where I stand, philanthropists are doing what they do — provide money to support and help groups, causes, and organizations that work with the needy, the poor, the homeless, and get tax benefits and positive publicity in return. Most of the nonprofits I have encountered are committed to helping people in need without posing intentional or unintentional harm. They feed the hungry, shelter the homeless, and provide other social services. People work hard, and many experience emotional and psychological fatigue connected to the work. However, my experience with homelessness and homeless advocacy work tells me that in order to end homelessness, there must be a shift from the approach of simply managing people without housing to also being proactive in embracing preventive measures, expanding the narrative about who is experiencing homelessness, and advocating for more low income and affordable housing. We must be willing to deconstruct the incentives that keep that from happening in the homeless industrial complex.

The sheltered homelessness system in the United States has reached a $12 billion dollar expenditure. None of that money has gone to providing permanent housing to the homeless or preventive measures, but rather to temporary solutions such as bag checks (lockers), day centers, public showers, and keeping the sheltered homeless machine going. All band aid solutions. That is a lot of money being spent not leading to permanent solutions. It reminds me of the "Prison Industrial Complex" in many ways. I thought about how incarceration had become big business in the United States due to connected industries, and exploitation of inmate labor. Prisons became entities for modern day slavery. I thought about how the privatization of prisons supported profit making. Now, I was beginning to see how it was happening connected to poverty and homelessness. Understanding that there will always be people experiencing homeless, too many of us have become too comfortable with the way things are, and not uncomfortable enough about why.

My friend and former colleague J. Bennett Guess, a minister and longtime social justice advocate, offered insight about charity. He spoke to charity being an honorable thing, but not if it is used to lift our story of self-righteousness, and in doing so impedes economic justice and social change. Through his words he introduced me to the martyred Archbishop of El Salvador, Saint Oscar Romero and his not calling people "poor" but "those made poor." It caused me to reflect on how we create and maintain the poverty around us, because it serves a purpose for someone in some way. How do we as individuals, members of groups, institutions, systems and society continue to make people poor? Ben said, "Throwing a few dollars, old clothes, or other to-be discarded stuff at the 'needy people' isn't the same as working, voting, and organizing for their liberation and systemic policy change." I agree.

It would not be until I read Robert Lupton's book *Toxic Charity: How Church and Charities Hurt Those They Help, And How to Reverse It* that I fully understood the social dilemma caused by good intentions of primarily well-meaning folks, the perceptions and myths held about poverty, the growing religious tourism industry, and the impact on those identified as poor and homeless in the U.S. and around the world. Lupton shares what he calls "The Oath for Compassionate Service" as a way for people serving and wanting to serve others to do so supporting their empowerment, dignity, and humanity. He explains 1) Never do for the poor what they have (or could have) the capacity to do for themselves, 2) Limit one-way giving to emergency situations, 3) Strive to empower the poor through employment, lending, and investing, using grants sparingly to reinforce achievements, 4) Subordinate self-interests to the needs of those being served, 5) Listen closely to those you seek to help, especially to what is not being said – unspoken feelings may contain essential clues to effective service, 6) Above all, do no harm.

Without a social change or social justice filter, well intentioned people get stuck on "doing good" and "feeling good" and "helping" people in need. People of faith connect their charity to ministry (or salvation), add service providers, careers and industries dependent on the situation, the lack of political will to develop and support policies or legislation that bring change, and things remain the same. We cannot change what we will not be truthful about. Asking what role our self-interest, religious beliefs and activities, the need to feel good, and political ambitions have in prolonging or ending homelessness is an important question to ponder. It requires the ability to view the issue objectively and a level of honesty that requires deeper reflection that leads to transformative action. What incentive is there to put an end to homelessness? There is little incentive to do anything transformative. We need a charity (address the current need) AND social justice (address what produces lack) mindset to address homelessness and its emerging issues to bring about transformative social change.

It is called an industrial complex because of the profit created from the social condition of homelessness and its emerging issues. When people lose housing, they often will need to place their belongings in a storage facility at a cost. Sometimes that cost overtime can become a burden, and they can lose those material possessions. When people are desperate to keep their housing, utilities on, or car running, they often will take a payday or title loan to meet that immediate need. The payday loan business sector, viewed as predatory lending, targets people in desperation which makes them susceptible to paying high interest rates. I remember taking my first payday loan, a second, third, and more. It was one of the survival mechanisms I saw working for me. I hit my brick wall when I was fired, and at the time of that firing I had two payday loans. I was able to negotiate with one company to pay them back. The other would not negotiate with me, and my credit was further impacted.

At the time I was living in Dover, Delaware. I moved there after accepting a case management position with Catholic Charities, Wilmington Diocese. It's interesting how getting that job came about. I went to Catholic Charities to get assistance with my electric bill. During the client intake I shared about my journey of being formerly homeless, and protracted search for full-time employment. I was told that there was an opening for a case manager, assured that I could be trained, and asked if I would consider the job. I would soon realize that my in-take was being done by the Basic Needs program manager, and she asked for my resume. I returned to the office that same day with my resume, and within weeks began training. I would be assigned to work in the Dover and Georgetown, Delaware offices, while living in Wilmington.

Working with Catholic Charities provided a needed perspective of life on the other side of the desk. It also provided insight into how and why people received help, and the enormity of issues and challenges connected to poverty, and the social services programs addressing it. It was the first job I had where I knew everyone that sat across from me was there because of a problem. A single mom with four children called for assistance with her utility bill. She was already in the system and was facing a disconnection. I was working her case so that she and her four children, each under twelve years old, would not be in the dark. She was frantic, so I flagged her case to management earlier in the week. She called me on that Friday, and I could not give her a definitive answer that she would get the help she needed. I was being told that she needed to wait. I was being shown to diminish my humanity and to embrace a level of indifference. I left the office that day knowing that there was the possibility that the client and her children would not have electricity that weekend. It was a rough weekend.

Each day, the client stories were a reminder of my days needing and seeking help. Some days were better than others, but all days highlighted the disparities in society. I experienced a mental and emotional weariness, and found myself questioning what I was doing, and processing why I was doing it. The ultimate measurement was gaining clarity about whether I was making the difference I wanted to make. Like Evelyn, I had to decide if my work made a real difference or was I another "hamster" on a wheel.

When my schedule called for me to work evening hours in Georgetown, the night drive became difficult. Getting to and from Georgetown while living in Wilmington involved driving through all three counties of the state, twice. During daylight hours, it was a time I utilized to decompress from the trauma of the day. However, the night drive was different. On my drive to Georgetown, located in southern Delaware (Sussex County) I would see confederate flags waving from cars or as stickers on vehicles. My sensibilities were heightened by the visual and the meaning it portrayed to me. I did not have the same sense of safety on the road at night that I had during the day. The days I worked evening hours, I also did not have the energy for the three-county drive home.

It would be then that my friend Retha provided a room in her house in Dover for me to stay when I worked late. I would not have to do the long drive from Georgetown to Wilmington. It was good to have full-time employment, and a friend looking out for me. The work at Catholic Charities would also solidify for me that my work connected with homelessness would not be with direct services.

After working with Catholic Charities for just over a year, I was eventually fired from my case manager position. I wasn't a good case manager. I wanted to help everyone and asked too many questions when I couldn't. I had a hard time saying no and keeping up with what seemed to be a growing need, without enough emphasis on prevention. As a case manager, I felt caught up in a vicious cycle focused too much on short-term remedies. Dependent on funding periods, people needing help got it, or didn't get it.

I'm reminded how frustrated I would be working as a case manager when I realized there was an expectation to get those seeking help into the office, even when there were no funds to help them. People would spend their last resources, face challenging situations to keep appointments, and sit at my desk, with me knowing that the answer would be no to their immediate need. I knew that I could not provide the help they were seeking, but I could not tell them until they were counted by sitting in the seat at my desk. That bothered me.

Two client experiences come to mind. A woman seeking assistance had an emotional outburst in my office. She did not understand how I could have her come in for help, and not be able to give it to her. Not because she did not meet the criteria, but because funds were not available. She was upset about me knowing I could not assist her, and not telling her. Her anger resonated with me, because it spoke to the issue of trust. I hated that I added to her trauma. The second was a middle-aged man who told me he had been everywhere looking for help. All he got was no after no. I remember thinking, all he needed was for someone to say yes, and although I wanted it to be me, it would not be. As I sat there listening to him pour out his frustrations and his pain, I knew I could not assist him. In both cases, my job that day was to get them in the office. I had done my part to oil the wheels of the homeless industrial complex by tying client count numbers to monies the organization received. I left that experience knowing that any work I would do connected to homelessness must be centered in advocacy. I now believe that it was the beginning of my gaining awareness of the homeless industrial complex, although I did not have the understanding or language to describe it that way at the time.

I understood that people were shut out of the process of obtaining decent, safe, affordable housing due to rising cost of rents, and the lack of low-income and affordable housing. People were at risk of losing housing due to low wages, loss of income, domestic violence, and evictions. People were denied housing due to fines, tickets and citations issued for life sustaining actions while homeless on the streets that showed up on background checks. People had difficulty finding housing due to past criminal offenses that came with housing restrictions once time had been served. People remain homeless due to the lack of permanent low-income housing being built. People become homeless due to the lack of preventive measures to keep them housed.

I am reminded of my own situation with eviction and saw prevention as key to ending homelessness. With prevention there would be less people experiencing homelessness to manage, and with less to manage, there would be a greater effect on meeting the goal to end homelessness. I saw the connection of the aforementioned to the homeless industrial complex, and I knew with all that we were doing, we needed to do better.

The loss of income placed me in jeopardy with paying my bills, which also impacted my ability to make timely rent payments. I began to struggle. I reached out to the Salvation Army in Dover, DE for rental assistance, and was able to get $500.00 toward my rent. During this time, I followed up a conversation that began a few years earlier with Sheree Hill-Manlove, an associate pastor at New Destiny Fellowship, the Wilmington, Delaware church I attended and that helped with my rent in 2011. Sheree had invited me to consider working with her company Positive Directions, which provided contracted school-based intervention services. I did not explore working with Positive Directions when first approached because I was so focused on remaining available to work in my field and was seeking full-time work that would provide benefits. I was an adult educator and thought that was where I held the most credibility in the field. I had never worked with children or teenagers in an educational setting. I went through the interview process and began working with Positive Directions as a part-time substitute behavior interventionist for the 2015-2016 school year across New Castle County Delaware. Although the position with Positive Directions was a part-time contract position, I worked consistently.

It was not lost on me that my saying yes to working with Positive Directions allowed me to keep a roof over my head and supplement my income to meet my financial obligations. Since I was driving across the bridge multiple times a week to work in New Castle County, I decided to move back to Wilmington, Delaware. I was able to find an apartment in a two-family house walking distance from Rodney Square in a section known as Greater Brandywine, near downtown Wilmington. It was an historical area known as a section of the city where African American professionals first owned homes. I would find out that some of the homes were still owned by members of those original families. There was an active community group. Periodically I would find community event information tucked in my door or mailbox. I did have the opportunity to meet some of my neighbors during a meet and greet for Bethany Hall-Long during her campaign for Lt. Governor at one of their homes. As a campaign supporter, Bethany invited me to meet her there. I simply walked around the corner.

The place I now lived was located two blocks down the street from the Wilmington Christina Care Hospital campus, around the corner and two blocks away from the Hotel Dupont which was near Market Street and Rodney Square. Most notable for me, the new apartment was walking distance from the homeless shelter I had spent those thirty life-changing days of my life. In the coming months, being that close to the shelter would serve as a reminder of the journey I was on.

HerStory Ensemble

I continued to work in the community with issues connected to homelessness. I began thinking more seriously about forming a group to promote and protect the rights of people experiencing homelessness. Coming out of my homelessness no such group existed in Delaware whose focus was on homeless legislation. It was important that the group bring focus to the plight of women, was proactive, empowering, and served the needs of those identified as formerly homeless, currently homeless, and at risk of homelessness. On a Sunday afternoon, the concept of HerStory Ensemble was formulated while I sat on the couch in the living room of my Dover, Delaware apartment. I will be the first to say that I did not know what I was doing, but sensed that whatever was happening, was something that needed to be done. In one afternoon, a website and email were created, and a phone number was identified. Within a few days our mission and vision statement would be developed. Our Facebook page would soon follow.

Our mission is to support the empowerment of women who have experienced homelessness by promoting awareness, education, economic development, and advocacy to end it. Our vision: attaining affordable, safe, and secure housing for all women. The mission and vision both embodied HerStory Ensemble as a community-based group lifting the empowerment of women impacted by homelessness, expanding the narrative about homelessness, promoting legislation that protected the humanity and dignity of people experiencing homelessness, and brought focus to the need for more affordable housing. HerStory Ensemble would emerge as an advocacy and empowerment community-based organization of women who had experienced homelessness, currently experiencing homelessness, or at risk of homelessness. We were the only community-based organization in Delaware primarily focused on and in the forefront of developing and promoting legislation to support and protect the rights of people experiencing homelessness. Our first task was to work toward the development of a homeless bill of rights for Delaware.

Over the next few weeks, business cards would be made, and I would begin to talk to friends and people in the community about the gap I saw in the work being done, and approach to homelessness that was not transforming, but rather stagnant, limited, and often oppressive. The concept for an organization like HerStory Ensemble came out of frustration and what I saw as a need for vulnerable people, with the lived experience of homelessness to have a meaningful voice in the systems set up to help them. It would be a tool for empowerment and engagement. I became frustrated working in community with individuals, groups, and organizations that refused to think outside of the box, and in doing so served as gatekeepers to change, and maintainers of the status quo.

There was much charitable work being done to address the needs of people experiencing homelessness. Charity met the immediate need but did little to address the lack of low income and affordable permanent housing or bring focus to elements of social justice regarding homelessness. As an advocate, I had yet to become aware of the industrial complex connected to poverty and homelessness. However, sexism and misogyny had made themselves known. I became weary of the power plays by male homeless advocates and community leaders I encountered. Their attitudes and behaviors indicated that they did not have a healthy awareness or respect for what I or other women brought or could bring to the table.

I remember a conversation with one person about working for homeless legislation in Delaware, where I walked away feeling disappointed because he questioned my motives. The impression the conversation left me with was, who was I to think that I could make a difference with legislation regarding homelessness? I was informed that people had been working on the issue of homelessness for years. He named a few people, asking me if I knew them. At the time being new to Wilmington's community activism connected to homelessness, I did not know many people. I knew none of the ones he mentioned. How much better it would have been for him to simply say "let me introduce you to some people." I left the conversation feeling as if he was saying "Woman who are you?" I will never forget how he made me feel. I now realize that what was lacking was a real sense of community that could have connected all of us in doing some important change work if we dared to.

The final straw was a conference call with some other community members I had worked closely with. I was accused of "betraying" the group by following through with steps to develop an agreed upon speakers' bureau (modeled after the National Coalition for the Homeless Faces of Homelessness Speakers Bureau in D.C.) in Delaware. Prior, I had travelled to Washington D.C. (on my own dime) to have a conversation with Michael Stoops. That visit and conversation provided insight toward the development of documents to assist the developing Delaware speakers' bureau. I'm still not clear what the tipping point was that precipitated the call; however, it was clear to me that there was a deliberate misinterpretation and misrepresentation of my actions. Reflection has led me to believe that my focus on results, clarity of purpose, and call for accountability, may have been problematic. After the call, I realized that I would never win any "pissing" contest. I simply did not have the necessary equipment. However, I did have a brain. These incidents were among those that shaped the niche and focus of HerStory Ensemble. Today, I thank those men for providing the incentive needed to establish an organization like HerStory Ensemble and in doing so, setting us apart. We were an organization primarily for and about the empowerment of women. We could not have done it without them.

Developing and leading a community organization was new for me. Having been a member of groups and organizations focused on social justice, I had come to understand the power of collaboration, making room for diverse perspectives, and knowing your vision, mission, and purpose. I also knew the need for members of groups to be empowered in the group. Another consideration was that I was a forced extrovert. I did not like being out front, and over the years as a member of groups had found satisfaction in supporting others while I remained in the background. I was more comfortable in the back of the room, rather than the front. I was a natural observer and astute listener. However, I had also experienced people interpreting that quietness or low-keyed behavior for weakness and timidity. Nothing could be further from the truth.

Establishing HerStory Ensemble forced me to push myself beyond my comfort zone. It pushed me to think more strategically about bringing the voices of people with the lived experience of homelessness to the conversations about homelessness. We envisioned an organization that honored the voices, collaboration, and sisterhood of women. Together, we could make a difference, and be empowered. It was decided early that HerStory Ensemble would not be a nonprofit organization, and that we would not receive any government monies. Initially, we would not have a brick or mortar location, but would be accessible through our website, our Facebook page, and other social media. There would not be a need for immediate paid staff because we did not provide any direct outreach or social services. The investment was people's time, and commitment to making a difference for self and others. These were cost savings decisions that allowed our funds to support the work and women in the community facing specific situations, and to put intentional energies into homeless policy and legislation work. The thinking was that the organization would explore ways to develop its own income and would be supported by the contributions of members and friends.

We needed an advisory board. As a diversity and inclusion specialist it was important to me that the advisory board reflect society. The vision was for HerStory Ensemble to have women who were close to the issue in various ways serve in this capacity. The women who came to mind each had a personal connection to me, a few I worked with professionally, and each brought diverse perspectives to the experience of homelessness, housing instability, and poverty. I first spoke with Rhonda, who I met when we were both residents in the shelter. She had also attended that large meeting of community stakeholders exploring a homeless bill of rights in 2012. We had maintained a friendship and communicated regularly about making a difference for people experiencing homelessness. During a conversation about the proposed work of the organization I asked her, "What makes us different?" and she replied "DeBorah, many people experience homelessness, most do not work for change."

I spoke with another friend, Shenandoah. We met as national staff doing racial equity and inclusion work for two different religious denominations and belonged to a group called the Ecumenical Justice Partners. I experienced her as an ally for the marginalized in society, and a person who wasn't afraid to ask questions of herself, and of others. After sharing my story and concept of HerStory Ensemble, she suggested that I check out another organization with a similar philosophy of empowerment, Thistle Farms. I learned about and was encouraged by Thistle Farms work with female survivors of domestic violence, human trafficking, and prostitution. Becca Stevens, its founder, was an ordained minister, a person of faith who wanted to do something different. It was refreshing to become aware of someone else focused on empowerment beyond charity. I thought about how Thistle Farm's social entrepreneurial model could work for the women of HerStory Ensemble as we moved forward.

Danielle was a co-worker and fellow case manager at Catholic Charities. She was in the audience with her colleagues in 2013 when I shared my story about homelessness, but we did not meet. She would be the person who got me acclimated to my work environment at the Georgetown, DE office when I started working there. Our discussions and her passion for children and youth in crisis informed me that she would be an asset to the work. I asked Danielle "Why did you say yes to serving as an advisor to HerStory Ensemble? She said "I never encountered anybody like you. You were the face of a cause. Your story was different for me, your perseverance, and HerStory Ensemble's work for change through legislation was different."

Rosemary was a friend I met at church and shared a connection through our faith community. She was familiar with the challenges and struggles of obtaining and maintaining housing, particularly for women and children living in transitional housing. Rose held a deep understanding and compassion about displacement and wanted to change how people viewed people experiencing homelessness. She said, "It can hit anyone, anywhere and anytime." Rose understood the need for people to approach the issue of homelessness in its broader context, beyond stereotypes.

Sherri worked with Delaware 's Community Corrections and was a community mediator for the Delaware Center for Justice. I met her on a more personal level through a mutual family friend at their masjid. We became friends and would connect in the community periodically. She cared deeply about people experiencing homelessness, particularly street homelessness, and would cook meals and drive around serving food. Her work connected her to adults and youth on the street, in correctional, and juvenile detention facilities. Sherri understood housing challenges for people reentering society also known as returning citizens, as well as women and families impacted by domestic violence. She understood the issue of homelessness from knowing and helping people who were experiencing it. Sherri shared that her "Strong belief in God and life's purpose are anchored on giving hope to the hopeless."

Minnie was a former colleague and sister/friend for more than twenty years. We met working at the Commission for Racial Justice of the United Church of Christ and became like family. My children knew her as Aunt Minnie. We connected around our social justice views and community work for social change. Minnie was a sociologist with a human services background. Her work and community experience involved working with nonprofits addressing injustices impacting families, children, youth, women, and people experiencing homelessness. She said, "It touched me that the work of HerStory Ensemble stood for social justice and empowerment."

Among the group were women of different faith traditions, ages, educational levels, life experiences, sexual orientations, and races. A core component of HerStory Ensemble's identity was having women who knew and understood the experience of homelessness, housing instability, and the important role of empowerment and advocacy to end it. We were not to be a religious or faith-based organization, or a charity in the sense of providing direct or social services. Our way of operating would be different because our work would be different. Every woman said yes without hesitation. We held our first conference call and began to explore the meaning and work of HerStory Ensemble in Delaware. HerStory Ensemble was positioned to be the only community-based organization of people with lived experience focused on homeless legislation in the State of Delaware. It was April 2015.

The limited cost incurred in setting up the organization was covered by my limited income. We did apply for a Neighbors In Need grant from the United Church of Christ. We received a letter dated May 20, 2015, stating "On behalf of The United Church of Christ and Justice and Witness Ministries, I am pleased to enclose a check for $1,000… to assist your organization with the justice work that you are undertaking." This was the first grant we had applied for, and it was the encouragement and confirmation we needed at the time that we were on the right track. Addressing homelessness was indeed justice work.

The early months of HerStory Ensemble were dedicated to building awareness about the group, and our work for a homeless bill of rights for the state of Delaware. I became the embodiment of HerStory Ensemble because of my story, my passion, and my willingness to share it. Our advisory board provided ideas, feedback for next steps, and their own stories supporting the quest to have a homeless bill of rights for the state of Delaware. I began to send emails and call people across Delaware to share what we were doing.

We were invited to be guests on the "Power Up with Dr. Marci Bryant" Show, a local cable television program. Danielle, Sherri, and I were guests on the program. Weeks later, we would appear on another program hosted by Wilmington City Councilman Justen Wright at the same cable network. That conversation led to a presentation before members of the Wilmington Delaware City Council. Each of these interactions provided exposure of the group's issues and purpose to fellow community members and political representatives. Our presentation before the Wilmington City Council resulted in a resolution by the city to support the Delaware Senate in its work in the development and passage of a Homeless Bill of Rights for the State of Delaware.

The members of HerStory Ensemble were provided more media opportunities to promote our mission, vision, and work. Minister Terrie Williams, host of "Time Out For Fore Play with Terrie Williams" on Heart Ministry Radio, and Pastor Brenda Divers, founder of Heart Ministry Radio and host of "Extraordinary People" provided space for deep conversations about homelessness and its emerging issues outside the political arena. I first met Terrie in community at a gathering where I shared my story shortly after coming out of homelessness. We would cross paths again when I worked at Catholic Charities. Her work there focused on veteran homelessness. Brenda welcomed me and HerStory Ensemble supporters a couple of times to share about community events connected to our work. Every opportunity we had to get people to expand their thinking about homelessness, who was homeless, and to get people to support homeless legislation was a gift and appreciated.

Beyond Charity

Before experiencing homelessness, I did not think much about the ways people could lose housing. I did not think about the systemic and structural barriers like negative background checks, sources of income, evictions (illegal or not), or the lack of housing that people could afford to rent. I did not think about the different levels of homelessness (street, sheltered/transitional housing or doubled-up/couch surfing). I did not think about approaches to homelessness, like the difference between managing the problem, preventing the problem, or ending the problem. I did not think about it.

I walked out of the shelter knowing that part of the solution to ending homelessness was to expand the thinking about it, and to move addressing it beyond the charity model. Going beyond the charity model called for eliminating stereotypes about homelessness and looking at the ways power and privilege connected to homelessness. That is, it called for acknowledging the full humanity of people experiencing homelessness, and identifying the ways we as individuals and participants in society's systems and institutions (social services, faith communities, law enforcement, political entities, families) oppress those who are not housed covertly and overtly.

We reached out to the National Law Center on Homelessness and Poverty, and the National Coalition for the Homeless, this time representing HerStory Ensemble. We were asked to serve as a Steering Committee member for the developing "Housing Not Handcuffs" campaign, and participated on monthly calls as part of an organizing group focused on activities connected to homeless bills of rights across the country and in Puerto Rico. The aim of the "Housing Not Handcuffs" campaign was to bring much needed focus to stopping the criminalization of homelessness and promote policies to end homelessness. The campaign facilitated us to enter our advocacy work with homelessness knowing from past experiences the importance of building trusted relationships and being in partnership.

We connected with legislators in Dover and began to help draft another version of a Homeless Bill of Rights for Delaware in the Senate. We were invited into the process to help shape this important legislation as people with lived experiences living in area shelters, transitional housing, in vehicles, and having been homeless on Delaware streets. The development of Senate Bill 134 was guided by legislative aide Leann Moore. She engaged HerStory Ensemble in the process with other community stakeholders by talking with us, meeting with us, and keeping us in the loop on the developing legislation. Senate Bill 134 sponsors and cosponsors were Delaware State legislators Sean Lynn, Stephanie T. Bolden, Bryan Townsend, Bethany Hall-Long, Margaret Rose Henry, Paul Baumbach, Robert Marshall, Harris McDowell, Helene Keeley, John Kowalko, John Mitchell, and Charles Potter, Jr.

Senate Bill 134 (SB134) titled "Homeless Persons' Bill of Rights" was heard in the Senate Community/County Committee of the 148th General Assembly May 18, 2016. The chairperson for that committee hearing was Senator Bethany Hall-Long. HerStory Ensemble along with other community stakeholders provided testimony regarding the bill. We invited Eric Tars, senior attorney with the National Law Center on Homelessness and Poverty, Washington, D.C. to frame the national movement regarding Homeless Bills of Rights (HBORs). I sat in the room almost overwhelmed by the task before us. HerStory Ensemble advisory board member Sherri Akil and my mom Margaret Whitfield were with me. Reminders of the hours of work, conversations with community stakeholders, and what the passage of this protective homeless legislation would mean for people identified as homeless flooded my mind. In that room, it was so evident that my experience with homelessness was so much more than about me.

We were witnessing the legislative process in motion. I spoke from the heart about protecting the rights of people experiencing homelessness, and was joined by a chorus of others around the room who shared their experiences of homelessness, and the need for a homeless bill of rights in Delaware. The room was full, the conversation was rich, and the bill was voted out of committee with pending actions to be taken before being presented for a full Senate vote. I left my first legislative exchange hopeful and trusting that people in the community experiencing homelessness had been heard, and that Delaware policymakers, and others who believed that people should not face discrimination based on housing status when seeking employment, services, or housing were one step closer to making that a reality.

It was only a few weeks earlier that HerStory Ensemble held its Empowerment and Advocacy Award Benefit to raise funds to support our work. Delaware State Representative Stephanie T. Bolden and Delaware State Senator Bethany Hall-Long attended and shared about Senate Bill 134. The Senator, a registered nurse and military wife had first connected to the issue of homelessness engaging homeless veterans. This would be the first time that Senator Hall-Long and I would connect on this important issue in the community, however, it would not be the last. Senator Hall-Long would run for Lt. Governor of Delaware in 2017 and win. I and members of HerStory Ensemble assisted with her campaign, and in doing so, helped to keep the issue of homelessness and housing insecurity in the forefront.

Fostina Dixon and Winds of Change, and our friend, storyteller Feather on the Wind (Theresa Randall) provided the evening's entertainment, another friend Donyale London Hall was our Mistress of Ceremonies. We utilized this time to highlight the work of Veronika Scott and The Empowerment Plan for providing people experiencing homelessness with coats that turned into sleeping bags, and for providing employment for people identified as homeless or formerly homeless. In the coming years Donyale would run for Delaware Senate and for Lt. Governor. I admired her spirit to bring change. Fostina Dixon, also known as the Saxophone Queen would continue to be a supporter of the mission of HerStory Ensemble and we would collaborate on other community events such as Peace Week Delaware, Justice Notes at the Delaware Art Museum, and the Fostina Dixon and Winds of Change Jazz Road Tour of Hope.

We were invited to do a presentation on Homelessness in Delaware for the Health, Aging & Disabilities Committee of the Wilmington City Council in May. It was an opportunity to lift our work for a homeless bill of rights in Delaware and to bring focus to the need for policies and practices to support people experiencing homelessness or at risk of homelessness. The presentation was followed by a discussion where the City Council decided to draft a resolution supporting the Delaware General Assembly Homeless Bill of Rights. The discussion was led by Councilman Justen Wright, who also sponsored the resolution with co-sponsorship of then Council President Theo Gregory, and Council Members Hanifa Shabazz, Sherry Dorsey Walker, and Maria Cabrera. The resolution was passed by Wilmington City Council on June 2, 2016.

A few weeks later, our legislative work in Delaware led to an invitation to participate on the "Changing Laws at the Local, State, and Federal Levels" panel at the National Forum on the Human Right to Housing in Washington, D.C.. Fellow panelists were David Pirtle (National Coalition for the Homeless), Diane Yentel (National Low Income Housing Coalition), and Don Sawyer (A Bigger Vision). It was my first-time meeting Diane and Don, however I had met David a few years earlier when he accompanied Michael Stoops to Delaware to meet with H.A.R.P. (Homeless Are Real People Too). I could not image that in the coming years, David and I would connect in community again, as members of the "Faces of Homelessness Speakers Bureau with the National Coalition for the Homeless. Now on the panel, I shared what we were doing to deepen awareness and understanding to address homelessness beyond direct services and charity in Delaware. The developing "Housing Not Handcuffs" campaign propelled us to explore policies and practices affecting people experiencing or at risk of homelessness, and the need to address the criminalization of homelessness. The importance of identifying allies and common ground was lifted through our relationship with the Wilmington City Council's support of SB134, and what that could mean for other cities across Delaware, and the nation. This would be our first national platform to share the work of HerStory Ensemble.

During the Summer of 2016 I had the opportunity to address the Executive Committee of the Delaware State Human Relations Commission. The Commission was identified as the entity to hear and decide grievances, and for enforcement connected to the Homeless Bill of Rights. My specific reason before this body was to discuss the growing criminalization of homelessness in Delaware, and to have the word criminalization included in the language of the pending bill. We were hearing about citations, fines, and arrests for activities that people identified as homeless must do in public because they had no place to go. Eating, sleeping, standing, camping, and parking, while perceived as homeless were being criminalized.

Again, it seemed so unfair and unjust to punish vulnerable people, particularly when they had no other place to go, and there was a lack of shelter beds for them to go to. I ended my time with the Commission with the following statement: "I seek your guidance and support for the inclusion of language in the Homeless Bill of Rights that speaks to criminalization as a form of discrimination based on housing status. I am trusting that we can work together for passage of a Homeless Bill of Rights for the State of Delaware that supports the total humanity and dignity of the people it has been developed to protect."

We continued to identify opportunities for deeper awareness and education regarding the criminalization of homelessness, the ongoing "Housing Not Handcuffs" campaign, and acts of marginalization impacting people experiencing homelessness. In November 2016 we reached out to other groups and organizations working with housing and homelessness issues to collaborate with planning the "Housing Not Handcuffs Community Justice Walk" in Dover, Delaware. The walk was pitched as an event that would serve as a public witness to the work and message of Dr. Martin Luther King, Jr. to be held in observation of King Day 2017 in the state's capital. A planning committee was formed with members of HerStory Ensemble and Victory Church, Dover, DE on behalf of the Community Voice Coalition. The Community Voice Coalition would be identified as a body of community groups and organizations in Delaware focused on social justice issues. Among community allies for the walk were NABVETS, DE, Nanticoke Council, Lanape Nation of Delaware, Black Lives Matter, DE, Port of Hope, DE, and the Delaware Hispanic Commission. We also had support from the National Law Center on Homelessness and Poverty, and the National Coalition for the Homeless, in D.C. On Saturday January 14, 2017, the Housing Not Handcuffs Community Justice Walk convened on Legislative Mall in Dover, Delaware. We were told that it was the first time such an event focused on homelessness had taken place there.

As a community-based organization of women with lived experience of homelessness and housing insecurity,

HerStory Ensemble was slowly turning the tide in getting people to see housing as a human right and expanding the narrative about homelessness. For me, this meant that there was a fighting chance with deeper awareness, education, and political will for the change needed to increase more low-income and affordable housing, and protect the dignity and humanity of people identified as homeless to come. It also was a message to the women involved that we were truly empowered to bring about social change in Delaware, and to collaborate with others across the country working for the same.

It would not be until the next legislative session that a second Senate hearing focused on a homeless bill of rights for Delaware would convene. The date, June 14, 2017. The lack of followup after the first hearing caused momentum to be lost. Many of us in the community felt betrayed and were disappointed. However, we were more determined than ever to continue the fight. The bill before us now was known as SB49, "The Bill of Rights for Homeless Individuals" and would again, serve to protect the human and civil rights of people experiencing homelessness. Senator Margaret Rose Henry was now chair of the Delaware Senate Judicial & Community Affairs Committee. Attorney Eric Tars with the National Law Center on Homelessness and Poverty could not make the hearing, but sent a letter highlighting key considerations which included economic advantages and the bill's support in ending the criminalization of homelessness upon passage.

The mood in the room was different. The time felt rushed. I remember feeling disheartened and frustrated as I listened to a representative from law enforcement present an argument that fed into the fear of and "public safety" arguments regarding people experiencing homelessness. A lawyer and representatives of a large service and shelter provider spoke to the need to have control over homeless residents and clients, painting all as dangerous, to be feared and needing to be monitored. In early 2017 we were made aware of LEAP (Law Enforcement Action Partnership). LEAP is an organization that consists of members of law enforcement who work with fellow law enforcement to expand awareness and understanding about controversial issues in the community, such as homelessness. We would discover that two of LEAP's members were retired Delaware law enforcement, and we were encouraged about having at least one of them to assist our efforts in addressing the resistance.

Both testimonies played into the fears and stereotypes needed to maintain the status quo. It was a distraction from the essence of the bill, protection of the rights people experiencing homelessness already had. The unwillingness of the service provider to not support legislation lifting the dignity, humanity, and human rights of people experiencing homelessness led me to their website. After visiting the site, I wrote a letter to the executive director asking a basic question, "Why would you not support a homeless bill of rights?" He responded with a letter inviting me to schedule a meeting for a conversation. We had a meeting with the organization's lawyer in the room. The same man that did his job at the bill's Senate hearing. I was not intimidated. I was not deterred. Nothing changed.

Prior to and after the hearing, HerStory Ensemble launched and maintained an aggressive postcard campaign for the passage of SB49. The postcard simply read "*Advocacy – To Change What IS into What Should BE*" on one side and on the other side read the following:

"Dear Legislator, . . .

As constituents we urge your support for the passage of a Homeless Bill of Rights for the State of Delaware. We believe discrimination has no place in our great state. Such legislation assures all people, regardless of housing status, equal opportunity to live in decent, safe, secure, and affordable housing, and provides protection of the humanity and dignity of people experiencing homelessness on every level while seeking housing, employment, and services. Thank you for your anticipated support of SB49."

There was space for the person's name, organizational information, and a required zip code. Cards were provided to community groups and organizations supporting SB49, and available at every community event HerStory Ensemble participated in as we sought support for the bill. Those that were not mailed, I would personally drop off. We sent postcards periodically to members of the Delaware House of Representatives and to the Delaware Senate to assist keeping the issue and pending bill alive. During this time, we received encouragement from an unlikely source, a group of fifth grade students from Elmer Palmer Elementary School in Wilmington, Delaware. Along with their faculty advisor Kelly Green and others, the group of young advocates made a trip to Legislative Hall in Dover, Delaware to meet with Senator Bryan Townsend and Senator Margaret Rose Henry about the Homeless Bill of Rights. A video of the visit showing the group engaging legislators and advocating for people experiencing homelessness was posted to social media. I and members of HerStory Ensemble were ecstatic.

Kelly worked with the National Liberty Museum in Philadelphia to bring the Young Heroes Program to their school. Young Heroes is a nine-week classroom curriculum that highlights children making a difference in the world and focuses on first amendment rights and social justice issues. The students chose to focus on homelessness. Kelly said "One thing that stood out for them was that many people defined a person by their homelessness. The students chose to advocate for person-first language, saying a person experiencing homelessness, instead of a homeless person." The students gathered signatures for the change, and support for SB49. The petition was presented to the two legislators. I would later meet with Kelly to thank her for her work to bring deeper awareness and understanding about the issue through the Young Heroes program at Elmer Palmer Elementary. I would learn that we both worked with Positive Directions but had never met each other. HerStory Ensemble and I were thankful for the advocacy efforts of some of Delaware's youngest citizens.

Despite our efforts, Senate Bill 49 died in committee. We would learn how protracted the legislative process could be. We would also be reminded of the importance of building a coalition of individuals and organizations with similar and related causes that fully understood the power in connecting and working together for the common good. Working for a Homeless Bill of Rights for the State of Delaware had garnered support from diverse groups and organizations. Among them were the State of Delaware State Council For Persons With Disabilities, and the League of Women Voters of Delaware, who either wrote a letter of support to legislators or promoted the effort through their membership network.

HerStory Ensemble continued to connect with others in the community bringing focus to homeless policies, practices, and legislation locally and nationally. I was invited to serve as a group facilitator for the Lt. Governor's community mental health and addiction forums scheduled for early 2018. As a social psychologist and daughter of a father who had lived with mental illness, I viewed it as an opportunity to have honest dialogue. In February 2018, I facilitated groups in Wilmington and Delaware City, respectively. Housing, homelessness, and the connection to mental health were recurring themes, as people living with mental illness are a most vulnerable sector of those identified as homeless. It was also an opportunity to assist in dispelling myths and stereotypes connected with homelessness, especially as someone who identified as formerly homeless.

A few months later I would be presented with the opportunity to move to Washington, D.C. I had to think long and hard about what relocating would mean for the groundwork we had done in Delaware, the continuity of having a community-based voice in the forefront calling for homeless legislation in Delaware, and what it would mean to do homeless advocacy in the nation's capital. The lease on my Wilmington, DE apartment ended and I would spend the last days of June living in D.C. before heading to the Society for the Psychological Study of Social Issues "Bridges To Justice: Building Coalitions and Collaborations Within and Beyond Psychology" conference in Pittsburgh, PA.

Months earlier a proposal was submitted for a session that would bring focus to the collaborative efforts of people in academia, law, and community advocacy working for rights of people experiencing homelessness. Dr. Ann Aviles, assistant professor with the College of Education and Human Development at the University of Delaware and author of *From Charity to Equity: Race, Homelessness and Urban Schools*, Eric Tars, senior attorney with the National Law Center on Homelessness and Poverty, and I presented the interactive discussion "Homelessness: Expanding The Narrative And Protecting Rights." I had the opportunity to be a guest lecturer a few times for Ann's class. This resulted in a group of her students producing a video on homelessness in Delaware. It was yet another time that I knew that the work of HerStory Ensemble was making a difference, particularly with young people. Over the years I had experienced Eric as an ally and continued to strengthen that relationship by supporting the annual National Right to Housing Forum in various capacities. We were able to present our diverse perspectives, experiences, and work addressing homelessness as an example for community engagement.

Now a Washingtonian, I got involved with community homeless advocacy as a member of the National Coalition for the Homeless Faces of Homeless Speakers Bureau. Since connecting with the National Coalition for the Homeless (NCH) years ago, I had maintained a relationship with them and wanted to be involved with their work in D.C. I knew that my story of experiencing homelessness was not unique, but my willingness to share it as someone who did not readily fit the dominant stereotypes and myths was. I would learn that my story was powerful, and when paired with fellow speakers, our combined stories provided a platform to expand the narrative about homelessness, support advocacy, and to promote self-empowerment. Hearing the stories of each of my fellow speakers the first time took me on a rollercoaster of emotions. Among members of the speakers' bureau are people who have experienced every level of homelessness, deep trauma, and extraordinary triumphs. The human spirit is truly resilient. As a member, I shared my story of homelessness and the advocacy work of HerStory Ensemble in Delaware, D.C., and surrounding areas. I represented the NCH primarily at area schools, universities, and with visiting church groups to the nation's capital.

Through the speaker's bureau I connected to other D.C. advocates and lobbyists which involved periodic visits to Capitol Hill as a group to meet with staff of legislators. The final event with the speakers' bureau for 2018 would be the observation of National Homeless Persons' Memorial Day. A somber reminder of all those who died identified as homeless on Washington, D.C. streets, or without permanent housing during the year. It was yet another time to lift the realities of homelessness.

We ended our work for the year with the first posting of the HerStory Ensemble blog. It took me back to the days of working with the *Civil Rights Journal* and remembering how important and necessary it was to connect in community by keeping in the forefront the issues of homelessness and housing. The overall goal was to have a space on our website in the coming year where community voices for advocacy and empowerment could be presented. The entry titled "Pressing Forward: HerStory Ensemble Protecting Rights of People Experiencing Homelessness" provided reflection on the ending year, shared news of my transition to D.C., our continued work in Delaware, and expectations for the coming year. I, and HerStory Ensemble entered 2019 hopeful and ready to embrace transformative change.

Empowered for Change

The work of HerStory Ensemble is hopeful work. Not only is it hopeful work, but it is transformative work as we look at homelessness and its emerging issues with an eye that sees what is, and an eye that sees what could be. We cannot do anything without hope, and that hope is given and supported by many things. My hope was often nurtured through my faith and belief that God was guiding my process, and that all I needed to do at the end of the day was to simply be obedient. Obedience meant listening to that inner voice, connecting with people I generally would not have, doing things that I never did before, and showing up at places and in spaces that I had not been.

However, January 2019 gave me reason to pause. That month I finished teaching my online university class and would have every subsequent class on my calendar after that one to be canceled. I would later learn that among other things, the university was changing to a different online platform that I would need to be trained on before teaching another class. In essence, I had been laid off, without directly being told so. I searched for the meaning in the experience, and what it was preparing me for. That easily again, lost income put my financial reality and housing in jeopardy in one of the most expensive cities to live in the United States. However, a notable difference this time, would be evidence of my ask of God years earlier to position me where my income did not depend on the will of others, had been answered. Those other streams of income provided me with money to pay my rent, keep my utilities on, and buy food. Thankfully, during this period I was able to meet my financial obligations. Within months, what I was experiencing personally would be a prelude to understanding the economic fragility of thousands of people across the district during the D.C. government shutdown, and job loss connected to the pandemic to come: Covid-19.

A conversation with my friend Iris prompted me to explore applying for unemployment benefits. She had been in a similar situation years ago after an out of state move. Following her suggestion, I was able to draw the maximum unemployment benefit from my online work while living in Delaware and its continuation in D.C., before the "lay-off." I also began to explore other income opportunities in the D.C. area, not knowing when or if I would be called back to the university. Receiving unemployment required that I register with the D.C. job search engine and report that activity weekly. I also signed with other search entities such as Indeed.com, Idealist, and Simply Hired. My friend Ann in Delaware sent me information about a director of policy and advocacy position in D.C. with an organization working with children and homelessness. I applied. Again, similar to my job search years earlier, no interviews were offered; however, I did attend two job search workshops. I would eventually be trained on the new online platform and offered a class. It would not be until May 2019, that I would again receive income from teaching.

My homeless advocacy work was now focused both in Delaware and Washington, D.C. That January I attended my first Delaware Continuum of Care General meeting. I was invited to the meeting by Carrie Sawyer Casey, Chair of the Board for the Delaware Continuum of Care, and Manager of the Division of Community Development & Housing, New Castle County, Delaware. Carrie and I first connected in community the previous year at HerStory Ensemble's "Housing Is Healthcare" community forum in observance of Hunger and Homelessness Awareness Week. For the last two years, HerStory Ensemble offered community empowerment forums highlighting a specific aspect of homelessness during this week of national observance lifting hunger and homelessness across the United States.

The first year we scheduled community showings and discussions of the film *the Pursuit of Happyness* at one library in each of Delaware's three counties to bring focus to childhood homelessness. The movie was inspired by the true story of Chris Gardner who survived homelessness and became a successful stockbroker. His autobiography was the genesis for the film. Both brought to the forefront childhood homelessness as an aspect of childhood trauma, and how homelessness can happen beyond the myths, and success can happen past the stereotypes. Community participation was poor. This second year we focused on awareness and advocacy connected to housing as a key element of healthcare. Carrie participated as a speaker on our Housing Remedies panel, where she shared about her work identifying, securing, and promoting low income and affordable housing. Gaining a deeper understanding of the work of the group, I left the January meeting a member of the Delaware Continuum of Care, and shortly became a member of its advocacy and policy committee. By the end of the year, I would be nominated and elected to the Delaware Continuum of Care board. I was assigned to serve as co-chair of the advocacy and policy committee 2020-2022.

HerStory Ensemble participated in the Westside Grows Martin Luther King Day Peace March in Wilmington, Delaware. This was our second year marching as a community organization to lift homelessness and its emerging issues. The event provided another opportunity to be in community connecting the message of Dr. King to the present-day struggles of people living in poverty. It was the coldest day; however, we would not be deterred by the temperature as we remembered the sacrifices of those who had come before us. We were stopped by a reporter with Delaware

Online, a local news outlet, and asked why we were there? Our response: "It's the least we could do to lift the realities of some of the people experiencing homelessness who deal with freezing temperatures and other inconveniences every day."

During the community celebration we were able to have a conversation with Delaware U.S. Senator Chris Coons, who stopped by our table. He shared with me about his work with homelessness as a young man in New York City, working with the National Coalition for the Homeless. A few months later, I would find myself on "The Hill" meeting with one of his staff members as part of a group of advocates lobbying for legislation supporting families living in poverty, and low-wage workers. I was representing the National Coalition for the Homeless. Toward the end of the year, Senator Coons and I would appear as speakers on the "Justice Matters For Everyone" program sponsored by the Delaware Combined Campaign for Justice.

The Delaware Combined Campaign for Justice consists of three organizations providing legal assistance to Delaware's poor. I was invited by the Community Legal Aid Society, Inc. (CLASI) to share my experience with a Delaware landlord to bring greater awareness to the need for legal representation and the right to counsel in tenant housing matters. The program also included a Delaware Supreme Court Justice, the Mayor of the City of Wilmington, and the Lt. Governor. I was listed as a Homeless Empowerment Advocate, and it was not lost on me that I was sharing my story as part of a lineup that included some of the most powerful people in the State. The program was held at a prestigious downtown law office located across the street from Rodney Square. The room was full of people, standing and in conversation with hors d'oeuvres and drinks in hand. It was an invitation only event. There were attorneys, politicians, community advocates and activists. I knew some of them.

My story began with having them imagining opening the door to a newly rented apartment and encountering an overpowering odor of cat urine. I talked about eventually discovering the odor permeating from the basement where cats had relieved themselves. I share how I immediately called the landlord, not getting an answer, I left a voicemail. I share how for two days, my multiple calls were not responded to, so I left a final message indicating that I had changed my mind about renting the apartment, had left the keys on the kitchen counter, and requested my money back. They heard about the landlord finally responding, saying that I had taken possession of the apartment, and that I was bound by the signed one-year lease. He also indicated that I was not going to get any money back.

I found myself in a vulnerable place. The decision to not live in a place that I deemed uninhabitable unleashed several considerations. First, I needed to find another place to live. Second, I would need to negotiate with my current landlord an extension to remain housed while looking for a place to live. Third, I had to figure out how to get my money back from an unreasonable and unresponsive landlord for an apartment that I would never live in. I decided to sue the landlord, without access to legal representation. I received guidance from friends who were familiar with the court system, but realized that the uncertainty, stress, and my lack of knowledge could have been lessened if I had counsel.

The story ended with me winning the case and receiving reimbursement of my money and payment of court costs from the landlord. I had walked through the fire as an advocate for self. This situation served to heighten my awareness about what people are faced with when for various reasons their backs are up against the wall when seeking remedy for situations related to obtaining and maintaining housing and having decent living conditions. I shared my story in a way that framed it to expand thinking about the vulnerability individuals and families experienced when dealing with housing issues and the court system. I wanted those in the room to see how easily situations and circumstances put people at risk of homelessness no matter their educational level or life experiences. They needed to understand how people can be made to feel powerless, and in doing so, accept unreasonable conditions, and are silenced.

Over the years, HerStory Ensemble's work entailed promoting the "Housing Not Handcuffs" campaign in Delaware with the National Law Center on Homelessness and Poverty. Our work was to locally remove unconstitutional panhandling policies currently on the books. The new "I Ask For Help Because" campaign aimed to shift focus to identifying why people would need to panhandle or ask for money, and push for eliminating the punishment mindset toward those needing to ask for that help. Both campaigns sought to stop people identified as homeless from being fined, arrested, or incarcerated for doing life sustaining activities in public. I would learn that it was not against the law to panhandle in Wilmington, DE, and that people who knew they would be involved in such activity for an extended period of time, could request a permit to do so. However, one could be arrested for panhandling after sunset or before sunrise.

Although I did not need to panhandle or ask anyone for money on the street, I knew from my experience with homelessness that there were many like myself who for various reasons could not check the boxes to get the help they needed from groups, organizations, or social services. Some would need to ask for help from strangers. One size has never fit all, and it never will when it comes to addressing homelessness. The ban and new campaign prompted members of HerStory Ensemble to request a meeting with the ACLU- Delaware after learning during a campaign conference call that they had been sent an invitation to join the campaign from the National Law Center on Homelessness and Poverty. We were the local community organization already working on this.

I reached out to my former colleague with the United Church of Christ, J. Bennett Guess, who was now the executive director of ACLU- Ohio, asking if he knew the director in Delaware. He did. Ben introduced Kathleen MacRea and me by email, and a meeting was scheduled. We discussed the Wilmington ban, the "I Ask For Help Because" Campaign, and offered HerStory Ensemble as a community resource. After the meeting, I introduced Kathleen and Eric Tars through email. The ACLU-Delaware would be involved with the campaign. Shortly after that ACLU-Delaware meeting I got an email from Daniel Atkins. The ACLU-Delaware had connected us. Attorney Atkins, executive director of the Delaware Community Legal Aid Society, Inc. (CLASI) approached me to join him as a co-guest on a local television program, "The Delaware Way" to address a recent ban by the City of Wilmington directed at a young man who had been accused of panhandling, an accusation the young man denied. "The Delaware Way" was a weekly local news/information program focused on what was happening across Delaware. HerStory Ensemble and other community members spoke out about the ban and its infringement on civil and human rights, its racial overtones, and criminalization of the poor and homeless. He asked that I bring a community perspective to "The Delaware Way" conversation about the ban. I said yes. We taped our segment to be aired early 2019.

In the new year, Dan would be instrumental in the participation of the members of HerStory Ensemble in a Delaware National Public Radio program focused on the state's high eviction rates. Our member Iris shared her experience with landlord retaliation for reporting unsanitary and unsafe housing conditions. Iris' story was representative of too many households in Delaware and across the country where renters must choose between having a place to live or settle for living conditions that put their health and safety at risk. Our collaboration with Delaware CLASI provided HerStory Ensemble the opportunity to use our sphere of influence to bring greater focus to homeless prevention by addressing evictions.

In D.C. the new year provided an invitation to the Congressional Briefing on Extreme Poverty: my first briefing on Capitol Hill. It was at this meeting that I gained a deeper sense of the issues and work being done connected to poverty around the world, in the United States, and in local communities. While driving home from that congressional briefing I viewed a man standing in the street, in the cold. Sitting in the second car stopped at a two-lane traffic light, I observed him approach the cars in both lanes in front of mine, asking for help. He was a frail African American male wearing oversized clothing, holding a small clear plastic cup which he held between his hands. His hands were placed around the cup, as if he were praying. He looked so broken. I watched him move between each car.

The image fits many stereotypes about "the homeless." Before he reached my car, I could feel the tears welling up. I reached into my pocket, lowered my window, and when he got to me, dropped the coins in his little cup. I heard him say, "Thank you." As the light changed, my thoughts went to the meeting I just left and the bumper sticker on my car "Everyone Deserves A Home" and I began to wonder about the man's story. He was someone's child. Possibly he was someone's brother, husband, or dad. What had brought this seemingly gentle man to ask for help on the street in the nation's capital on this cold winter day? I wondered if I was witnessing humility, defeat, or both. By the time I made the turn onto my street the tears were rolling, and I thought, we must do better. My coins may have helped him this day, but they did nothing for the broader change needed. I was reminded that charity was not a useful weapon in battles for social change.

Beyond Charity

The month of February found me co-facilitating a discussion with fellow members of the National Coalition for the Homeless at the National Anti-Hunger Policy Conference in Washington, D.C. The discussion's goal was to assist service providers and outreach organizations across the nation to explore utilizing people with lived experiences in their work in more innovative and empowering ways.

The keynote was Delaware State Representative Lisa Blunt Rochester. I was excited because I had made dozens of calls on her behalf as a volunteer with the Democratic Party office in Wilmington, DE, and was proud to have played a part in making Delaware history with her election. I reached out to a mutual friend asking that she let her know that at least one of the people in the audience was from Delaware and had voted for her. That resulted in her giving me a shout-out and thanks during her remarks. I was pleased to find out that there were other Delawareans in the room representing the Delaware Food Bank. It was a good day.

During Women's History Month, my daughter Jasmine and I would drive to Chicago to participate in a community program focused on women overcoming challenges. The invitation was made by Dr. Wanda Evans-Brewer, a fellow educator whose story of needing to secure public assistance to support her child while working as a university professor was featured in a documentary highlighting the pay inequities in higher education. I knew the struggles of trying to make ends meet while underpaid. Months earlier I was made aware of Wanda's story while doing research and connected with her on Facebook. Although she was never homeless, we both lived with the inconsistencies of being Black, female, and educated in the United States. That was enough. We eventually talked and became kindred spirits. This event would be the first time we met in person, and she and her young daughter Gia extended their hospitality toward us. We joked that "Good things can come from Facebook." It helped develop our friendship and sisterhood through our advocacy work.

Over the next few months, I would be afforded speaking engagements through the Faces of Homelessness Speakers' Bureau sharing my story of homelessness and advocacy with groups and organizations in D.C., and outside the district. My first outreach run would be with a group of young people from Southold Presbyterian Church, located in Southold, New York. A fellow speaker and I accompanied the group to Dupont Park where they engaged people in the park by handing out sandwiches, bottled water, and a kind word. A few weeks later I received a note card from their pastor. On the walk to the park, he and I realized during our conversation that we knew some of the same people associated with the Presbyterian Church (USA). Rev. Dr. Peter Kelley thanked me for my ministry and for utilizing my story to, as he said, "effect change in a most vital area for God." It confirmed that I was indeed on purpose and on the path for transformative change.

Two packets arrived. One was sent certified mail, and the other was left at my apartment door. At first, I did not know what I was looking at, but eventually realized I had just received notice that the apartment complex I was now living in was up for sale. I had only been a tenant for nine months at the complex and loved my apartment. My building had 4 one-bedroom apartments. Our apartment complex was in a section of D.C. known as Southeast, near the Maryland border. It was a quiet building with all African American tenants who worked. Eventually, my neighbors and I received notice of a community meeting to discuss the sale and our rights as tenants. I knew that I would be there. I did not think that there was any other choice.

The community meeting was held at the public library, which was walking distance from the complex. That evening I learned that the packet we received was an offer to tenants to purchase the property. We were also informed that a company had already indicated interest. There were 110 rental units, of which 106 were occupied, and a multi-million-dollar price tag. As residents of a multi-dwelling property being sold in Washington, D.C., we had the opportunity to buy it under TOPA (Tenant Opportunity to Purchase Act). However, we needed to be organized as a tenant association to participate in the process. We were not.

It would be an understatement to say that I was growing weary of the close calls with housing insecurity. Before relocating to D.C. I was aware of the wave of gentrification, and its connection to displacement and homelessness. Now, my fear was that the new owner would buy the complex and turn the property into condos, pricing many of us out. My anxiety rose when only eight units were represented at the community meeting. I could not believe the level of apathy among the residents, but knew that we needed to get many others involved to have input about the future of the property, which translated for me to protecting and securing housing.

The community organization convening the meeting suggested that we could do one of three things: nothing and let the process proceed with the group that had indicated interest, and not evoke TOPA rights; form a tenant association to enter the TOPA process to buy the property ourselves; form a tenant association to enter the TOPA process to have input regarding who would buy the property and to present tenant conditions for the sale. We decided to form the tenant association that night. We needed a percentage of the residents to be members of the tenant association to be incorporated.

My next door neighbor left the meeting as the interim president. A resident from a building across the street from us was the interim vice-president, and I reluctantly accepted the position of secretary. My plate was already full with other obligations and other community activities in Delaware and D.C., and I was focused on completing the writing of this book. I did not want the responsibility or accountability associated with the position, or the anticipated uphill battle convincing fellow tenants to be a part of the process. The next few weeks we knocked on doors to obtain support and signatures for the developing tenants association, held informational meetings, and learned more about the TOPA process. The tenant association was incorporated within the following months. I could now add tenant organizing to the list of advocacy efforts.

The community engagement of HerStory Ensemble helped us to bring that deeper awareness and education about homelessness and its emerging issues we sought. Personally, I was energized by each opportunity to expand the narrative about homelessness. I was grateful to build relationships with people, groups, and organizations connected to preventing and ending homelessness. The move to Washington and continued advocacy work in Delaware positioned HerStory Ensemble and me to work on homelessness and emerging issues on the national, state, and local level. I found the political and community advocacy climate in Washington D.C. to be more aggressive and outspoken, in comparison to the conservative culture of Delaware. As a native New Yorker, it was refreshing to see people speak truth to power. Unlike Delaware, on any given day somebody or some group is protesting about something in D.C., so there is consistent energy lifting various issues, and calling for social justice and change.

I remember thinking as it related to homelessness, I left a "pond" in Delaware and entered a "river" in D.C. The visualization of that reality hit me early one morning as I arrived by Uber at Union Station to catch an early morning bus to New York City. I walk through a row of bodies — people sleeping outside the station with their belongings. There were other bodies scattered around the entrance of the station. As I entered the station, I was asked by a security officer where I was going, once told he wanted to see my ticket. It was then that I realized that the number of people outside the station was so great because they were not allowed to be in the station during the overnight hours. I proceeded to my bus thinking with each step this is just not right.

People should not be sleeping on the streets at Union Station in the shadow of the U.S. Capitol. The visibility of the problem and the disparity it represented was enormous given the backdrop of its existence in the nation's capital. As the bus rolled out of the station, I found myself reflecting on what I just witnessed, the belief that housing was a human right, and the work of HerStory Ensemble for homeless legislation. All of us truly working to empower people experiencing homelessness and at risk of homelessness did not have the option to give up. HerStory Ensemble would continue the fight in Delaware and in D.C. We knew what it felt like to be empowered for change.

We Matter

For several years HerStory Ensemble has used the hashtag #WeMatter. We started using #WeMatter as a way to humanize people experiencing homelessness, and to be in solidarity with the message and mission of the Black Lives Matter Movement. People with particular identities in society, such as those identified as Black, poor, or homeless experience similar prejudices and criminalization. Another connection was the understanding that although African Americans counted as 13% of the U.S. population, recent reports indicated we were 50% of people experiencing homelessness on some level (street, shelter, transitional housing, doubled-up with family members). It was important wherever we found Black people facing oppression, marginalization, or brutality to proclaim that Black Lives Mattered. It was equally important for people experiencing homelessness, formerly homeless, and at risk of homelessness to proclaim, "We Matter."

The heightened cry of Black Lives Matter resulting from the murders of George Floyd, Breonna Taylor, Rayshard Brooks, and the many others before them at the hands of law enforcement, leads us to expose and to stop police brutality where we find it. The beating of a handcuffed man identified as homeless by a member of the LAPD (Los Angeles Police Department) was also caught on tape, as well as the assault and arrest of a wheel-chaired man identified as homeless during a Black Lives Matter protest by the same police department. We cannot be naïve to believe that Los Angeles is the only city where people identified as homeless are experiencing police brutality or harassment. We know that the criminalization of homelessness is a daily reality in too many cities across the United States. This makes the call for "Housing Not Handcuffs" more relevant than ever, and brings deeper reflection on society's law enforcement, court, housing and homeless services systems, and the role of race and racism in each of them.

History tells us that housing justice is racial justice, and so we must continue to fight against policies and practices that keep people out of housing due to their skin color, their source of income to pay rent, or maintain the lack of low-income and affordable housing. We cannot forget redlining, blockbusting, and a banking system that did not support Black people and others who were not identified as White. When I started my homeless advocacy journey, I caught a glimpse of the impact of race and racism in homeless services. I saw it in who was at the table making the decisions and leading local and national organizations, who was running major charity programs, and who was on the receiving end of services. There was a "Sea of Whiteness" and a culture that was heavily paternalistic among service providers. My years of experience doing antiracism, diversity, inclusion, and equity work had burned me out. I reached the point where my thinking leaned more toward people not having the will to do the necessary hard work, even when they had good intentions. After all, I had done this work with church folks, and it was some of the hardest work I would ever do.

Although I was no longer facilitating antiracism, diversity, inclusion and equity workshops or sessions, I found myself dealing with all the emotions, challenges, and misinformation that work encompassed teaching sociology classes at the University of Phoenix. Each class brought to the forefront how diverse our thinking was about issues connected to privilege and oppression, and how both showed up in lived experiences among diverse groups of people. From class discussions about Native American mascots and the changing of racist team names like the Washington Redskins, Cleveland Indians, and retiring the image of Chief Wahoo, to White privilege, and the difference in policing within Black communities, our historical and current prejudices, biases, and racism were exposed and explored.

I did not want to deal with race and homelessness. My work connected to homelessness was shaped to support the humanity, dignity, and rights of people identified as homeless, no matter their racial identity. I understood that race was an important factor in addressing homelessness, but I did not see, or maybe did not want to see it directly as part of the work I believed I had been called to do. My plate was full simply getting people experiencing homelessness to be viewed and treated as human beings with all the rights and privileges as housed people. My work centered around the group identity of people experiencing homelessness and not racial identity. I approached the work fighting against discrimination based on housing status. I cannot express the relief I felt when the SPARC Report, an acronym for Supporting Partnerships for Anti-Racist Communities, a racial equity resource exploring racism and homelessness was released.

The 2018 report shared how Blacks were more likely to experience homelessness, and how systemic racism and discriminatory practices supported disparities in service programs geared to people experiencing homelessness and obtaining permanent housing. The report also looked at the overwhelming representation of Whites in leadership, decision making, and jobs connected to the housing and homeless services systems. In 2020, that report and the current events of the day serve as a reminder of how race and racism permeated all areas in society,

The government shutdown in 2019 and now, the Covid-19 Pandemic of 2020 served as reminders of the steps I had taken when I lost income, could not find work, and was eventually evicted. I knew up close and personal what it felt like to live with limited income, visit food pantries, seek social services, and live with the risk of homelessness. Living in Washington, D.C. during the government shutdown exposed how vulnerable those not identified as poor were. My daughter, a government employee and I talked about the newness of her possibly not having enough money to pay bills. In her young adult life, she had yet to experience living from paycheck to paycheck, or seriously budgeting as she now was forced to do. As I looked at news story after news story about the furlough, watched people line up around "The District" for food, and heard the growing concern about meeting basic needs, it became evident that the situation presented an opportunity for people to expand their thinking about poverty, those identified as poor, and further examine our perceptions and judgments about those with economic challenges.

The Covid-19 pandemic provided yet another opportunity for not only D.C. residents to revisit economic and equity challenges, but to highlight specific challenges for people experiencing homelessness across the country. Being asked to shelter at home when you do not have housing, social distance while living in homeless shelters, on the streets, and encampments, or to practice preventive and life-saving hygiene with limited or no access to sanitation options, presents overwhelming challenges for individuals and communities. There was a greater sense of urgency among homeless advocates to have housing that protected the health and well-being of people experiencing homelessness during the pandemic.

As a member of the D.C. Covid-19 Policy/SAVE(Strengthening America's Values and Economy) For All Working Group, I was able to follow developments with each of the CARES (Coronavirus Aid, Relief, and Economic Security) Act packages. Our weekly Zoom calls discussed what each plan entailed, where improvements could be made, and what we needed to do as organizations, groups, and individuals to have each package address the needs of society's most vulnerable. I was introduced to SAVE through my association with the National Coalition for the Homeless (NCH). I periodically attended monthly issue meetings with associates from NCH and connected with other SAVE members on legislative visits on Capitol Hill.

My engagement with SAVE and the Covid-19 Policy Working Group opened my eyes more to how important each person's voice and vote is to our democracy. It often felt like I was in a masterclass, listening and watching longtime lobbyists speak to the issues of the day. Walking the halls of the legislative buildings in D.C. brought to the forefront for me the awesome responsibility and accountability our U.S. senators and state representatives have to us in developing policies and laws that are just and equitable for all members of society. This was especially true in addressing the needs of those identified as poor, homeless, and otherwise vulnerable. My community advocacy has led to questions about my political aspirations. I find politics to be messy, but necessary. It is clear to me that my role is one of advocate, activist, and change agent. It is a role I see played out in community alongside people living with the issues, rather than in public office. I do appreciate those who enter the political ring who keep their constituents in the forefront, and not for their own personal and political gain. We need legislators that hear the concerns of all constituents.

In the community I pressed for people to connect with their legislators and to participate in the political process on every level. I saw the power in voting. Many years ago, I heard community activist Margaret Ellis, a fellow staff person with the Commission for Racial Justice in North Carolina speak to the importance of connecting the breadbox to the ballot box regarding the need to exercise the right to vote, and the power it provided for us to have a say in the policies and laws governing our lives every day. I still consider it to be a great analogy. I continue to learn about politics and homelessness in Delaware, recognizing that there is a political component to everything in life. Lobbying for tax credit for low-wage workers, increase in SNAP benefits for low-income households, and reaching out to state legislators to fully support components of the CARES Acts that specifically targeted families, housing, and people experiencing homelessness keeps me involved in necessary legislative and advocacy work nationally and in Delaware.

I received an email asking for a meeting. Christian Willauer, a community activist with connections to civic associations in the City of Wilmington, the Wilmington Neighborhood Coalition, and the H.O.M.E.S. (Housing, Opportunity, Mobility, Employment, Stability) Campaign, wanted to discuss rental conditions in Wilmington and how we could work together. She shared with me ideas, and advocacy being done at the grassroots level to help people who were homeowners, renters, returning citizens, and to provide more low-income and affordable housing. She had my attention. Homeowners in Wilmington were at risk of losing their housing due to high water bills. Often, the people in these situations were senior citizens. People released from jails and prisons in Delaware were more than likely not to have permanent housing. That conversation allowed us to brainstorm about a grassroots community meeting focused on housing and homelessness, and other connected community issues.

The Wilmington Housing Summit convened February 2020, cosponsored by Network Delaware, Coalition to Dismantle the New Jim Crow, and the Metropolitan Wilmington Urban League. Members of HerStory Ensemble were in attendance, and I co-facilitated the session on homelessness. Through the process I would meet Shyanne Miller, who served as leadership with the H.O.M.E.S. Campaign and be introduced to members of the Building People Power Campaign (a second grassroots movement in Delaware working with similar issues). I would reconnect with my friend Dr. Ann Aviles from the University of Delaware, who was working closely with the developing H.O.M.E.S Campaign.

During the same time, I received a text from Lt. Governor Bethany Hall-Long. She wanted me to know that a 2020 candidate for the Delaware State Senate would be contacting me to talk about my advocacy work connected to a homeless bill of rights for Delaware. A few days later I would have a conversation with Kyra Hoffner. Kyra was involved with homeless outreach and wanted to do more for the people she crossed paths with who were unhoused. She was interested in pursuing passage of protective and supportive homeless legislation in Delaware. I had not totally given up hope for a homeless bill of rights and was pleasantly surprised. I welcomed the opportunity to work with anyone who was sincerely committed to reaching that goal. Kyra and I met before the Wilmington Housing Summit. She was already aware of the event, and I encouraged her to attend. She did, spending most of her time listening to community members and proposed suggestions on how to better address homelessness in the city.

HerStory Ensemble and I formed a collaborative bond with the H.O.M.E.S Campaign as members of its Unhoused Team. It would be within this team that the conversation to secure a homeless bill of rights for Delaware would again resurge in community. As a member of the Unhoused Team of the H.O.M.E.S. Campaign, I felt a sense of solidarity with people who understood the work we were doing as a matter of justice. Housing was a human right. People without housing should not face discrimination due to their housing status. Much had not changed from 2012, 2015, or 2017 connected to homelessness in Delaware. There continued to be a growing need for a homeless bill of rights, and homeless prevention. The collaboration would connect us in advocating for people experiencing homelessness during Covid-19 in Delaware. Sign-on letters were sent to the Governor, an ask for more motel/hotel vouchers to assist with quarantine in place orders was made, and the request for data collection for people contracting and/or dying from Covid-19 identified as homeless. I learned a long time ago that as a society we measure what is important to us.

Early summer 2020, in the midst of the Covid-19 pandemic, daily protests across the country tackling systemic racism, police brutality, pending evictions, and continued criminalization of homelessness, a new conversation about homeless legislation was happening in Delaware. What started as a question in 2012 and was proposed legislation that died in Delaware legislative committees in 2014 and 2017, was now in 2020 being looked at again. The renewed interest and energy in securing a homeless bill of rights caused me to reach out to Leann Moore. No longer a legislative aide, she still was involved in addressing community concerns, and like me, held the historical memory needed to inform the process. Leann's experience and knowledge would prove invaluable as we sought to engage current and new Delaware legislators.

HerStory Ensemble collaborating with the H.O.M.E.S. Campaign could facilitate the empowerment of more community members to participate in the process of stopping the criminalization of homelessness and working for more homeless prevention in Delaware. Having a political candidate like Kyra Hoffner helping to lead the change was encouraging. A politician was reaching out to the community about housing and homeless legislation, and that was different. She already was engaging legislators and others in the process as possible allies. We were slowly forming a core group of people to begin the work again. The plan was to introduce the new homeless legislation in early 2021. Our first review of the last version of a proposed Delaware homeless bill of rights provided a sign that we were on track. Leann was in the process of going through the last version of the bill to change its language to person- first language. The new legislation would represent what the Young Heroes from Elmer Palmer Elementary had advocated for as confirmation of the humanity of people experiencing homelessness. I would be looking to see where we could strengthen protections against the criminalization of people experiencing homelessness, and exploring how to better address the misinformation, fears, and power dynamics surrounding the legislation. This time it felt different. There was a real possibility for transformative change, and that was the hope.

My homeless advocacy work over the years has continued to promote homeless prevention and to call for those making decisions impacting the lives of people experiencing homelessness to be more responsive to meeting the needs of people without housing. In late July 2020 I was invited by the National Coalition for the Homeless (NCH) to partner with members of a consulting group working with HUD (U.S. Department of Housing and Urban Development). I along with others through NCH were to assist in the development of resources that included onboarding videos for various staff positions for groups and organizations receiving HUD funds addressing homelessness and COVID-19. HUD wanted people with the lived experience of homelessness to partner with its consultants to provide valuable insights about existing programs like rapid rehousing, environmental concerns and considerations connected to emergency shelters and other housing options supported by HUD funds, among other things. My experience working for two denominations and as a university professor provided an opportunity for me to write and expand curriculum for workshops and class modules. Now, I was involved in writing a curriculum for HUD workshops that would serve continuums of care, agencies, and grass-root organizations in their homeless services work.

DeBorah Gilbert White, PhD.

I accepted this opportunity to facilitate transformative change from the national level. It caused me to reflect on how far my advocacy had brought me. I could not have known that first night lying on that top bunk in a Wilmington, Delaware homeless shelter that the journey would lead to where I was involved with having an integral part in shaping equitable practices, policies, and relationships for homeless service providers. My first HUD engagement had me providing a racial equity lens to support Emergency Solution Grants components (street homelessness outreach, emergency shelter, homeless prevention, rapid rehousing, and the homeless management information system) for people who would be doing the work. It was a perfect fit for someone who exited homelessness knowing the importance of providing people with what they needed and protecting the dignity and humanity of people identified as homeless. The HUD contract paid more each hour worked then I had earned hourly my entire work-life. I now knew for sure what my experiences were all about and how I had been prepared for the work at this moment. Sometimes we think our education and experiences have prepared us for one thing, when they served as the foundation for something else.

The journey through homelessness and its aftermath taught me how fierce a battle it is to dare to ask different questions, have greater expectations, and hold those in power accountable for their treatment of people who hold stigmatized identities in society. People living with mental illness, people living in poverty, people experiencing homelessness, and other vulnerable groups, continue to have hope that the day will come where we all will have what we need from a society that values fully who we are. I still teach my sociology classes, but unlike ten years ago, students are asked to share about their community involvement. In essence, they are asked to think about what they are doing to make the world better in their own spheres of influence. They are being asked to consider whether they are part of the problem or the solution. They are asked to consider where they can take a stand for social justice and social change. I believe that every experience we have in life, if we are paying attention equips us for our purpose. I am resilient. What could have destroyed me on so many levels, has made me stronger. There are many of us in that number, and I have crossed paths with some of you. Let us not give up in the fight for social justice and social change, no matter what it looks like!

ABOUT KHARIS PUBLISHING

KHARIS PUBLISHING is an independent, traditional publishing house with a core mission to publish impactful books, and channel proceeds into establishing mini-libraries or resource centers for orphanages in developing countries, so these kids will learn to read, dream, and grow. Every time you purchase a book from Kharis Publishing or partner as an author, you are helping give these kids an amazing opportunity to read, dream, and grow. Kharis Publishing is an imprint of Kharis Media LLC. Learn more at https://www.kharispublishing.com.

www.ingramcontent.com/pod-product-compliance
Lightning Source LLC
Chambersburg PA
CBHW070157100426
42743CB00013B/2939